Solving Cryptic Crosswords

by Denise Sutherland

T0385740

Solving Cryptic Crosswords For Dummies®

Published by

John Wiley & Sons Australia, Ltd
42 McDougall Street
Milton, Qld 4064
www.dummies.com

Copyright © 2020 John Wiley & Sons Australia, Ltd

The moral rights of the author have been asserted.

ISBN 978-0-730-38470-0

A catalogue record for this book is available from the National Library of Australia

Cover image: © izzet ugutmen/Shutterstock

Typeset by SPi

Printed and bound by CPI Group (UK) Ltd, Croydon, CR0 4YY
C9780730384700_150525

The manufacturer's authorized representative according to the EU General Product Safety Regulation is Wiley-VCH GmbH, Boschstr. 12, 69469 Weinheim, Germany, e-mail: Product_Safety@wiley.com.

Contents at a Glance

Introduction

People love to do puzzles of all kinds; word squares, anagrams, number puzzles, riddles, conundrums, jigsaws and so on have entertained and educated people everywhere for thousands of years. And, since 1913, crosswords have held sway! In the mid-1920s some devilish brutes in England warped the more clear-cut original crossword from the United States, devising the cryptic crossword, where each clue — rather than being a synonym for the answer — was a tiny puzzle in itself. Since then, this fiendish variation of the crossword has spread through the Commonwealth, and more recently to the United States, to perplex, tease and delight millions of fans.

However, to anyone new to cryptic crosswords, delight may be rare! On first reading, cryptic crossword clues look like complete and utter gibberish (you call *that* a clue?!). This is where this book comes in. Cryptic crosswords conform to a set of rules and they *can* be solved. Honest! My goal is to be a friendly guide on your journey into this new territory.

I have wanted to write this book for many years, and I am thrilled to finally be able to share it with you. I remember all too well my first stumbling passes at cryptic clues, the confusion (which I still feel at times!), and how many years of practice and failed attempts it took to get to the point where I could not only solve cryptic clues, but also write the perplexing things. I hope that my explanations help turn the befuddlement you feel now into clarity and success when trying cryptic crosswords for yourself.

About This Book

My goal in writing this book is to give you a clear guide on how to decipher cryptic clues, without any intellectual 'snobbery', and set you on the path to cryptic crossword mastery.

In this book I give you an introduction to cryptic crosswords, provide you with a great set of tips for how to get started on any crossword (even if you can't solve any of the clues!), and a set of cryptic solving strategies. Most importantly, I take apart the main clue devices, one per chapter, and give you small teaching crosswords, along with explanations for each and every clue in these crosswords (and the answers!).

Note: While I've done all I can to provide you with the tools and information you need to solve cryptic crosswords, true proficiency only comes through practice. Despite all the theory in the world, to get a grip on this challenging puzzle genre, you really need to have a go at cryptic crosswords regularly.

Conventions Used in This Book

A few conventions are used in this book, which you need to be aware of:

>> I use *italics* to indicate any words from a clue.

>> I use ALL CAPS to indicate the answer to a clue, or set of letters that form part of the answer.

>> I also use *italics* when I introduce a new concept or technical term.

>> The *definition* means a synonym or definition for the answer.

>> The *wordplay* means the cryptic device and fooling around with letters that provides another way of getting to the answer.

>> An *indicator* is a word in a cryptic clue that indicates, or signposts, the sort of wordplay being used.

>> The *Chambers Dictionary, Shorter British Oxford Dictionary* and *Australian Oxford Dictionary* are my standard reference books.

>> I occasionally use American spelling in a clue, if this is necessary to get an anagram to work, but otherwise this book and the clues are in Australian English.

>> In a few places you see references to websites; these web addresses are set in monofont like this. If a URL runs across two lines, I've not added any extra spaces or hyphens to the web address, so just type it in to your web browser exactly as it appears in the text.

>> Any text in a sidebar (which is in a shaded box) isn't essential reading, and you can safely ignore it. The text in these is just an interesting aside to the main text.

Foolish Assumptions

I haven't made many assumptions in this book; the main one is that you have some interest in learning to solve cryptic crosswords! I do also assume that you have a basic knowledge of grammar (understanding the difference between nouns and verbs, for example, and what plurals, synonyms and adjectives are). But that's about it.

How This Book Is Organised

Solving Cryptic Crosswords For Dummies is divided into four parts, as follows.

Part 1: Diving Into the World of Cryptic Crosswords

This part consists of eleven chapters. The first chapter gives a basic introduction to cryptic crosswords in general, defines what makes up a cryptic clue, and explains the terms and conventions used in crosswords. It also delves into the history of crosswords a bit, in a sidebar.

The next eight chapters (Chapters 2 to 9) tackle the main cryptic clue devices you come across in these crosswords, from anagrams and linked words through to deleted letters and double definitions. Chapter 10 discusses ways that single letters, or very short words, are clued in all cryptic clues (regardless of the wordplay device being used). Part 1 finishes up with a brief discussion about cryptics around the world.

Part 2: Sample Cryptic Crosswords

This part of the book has three chapters of practice cryptic crosswords for you to get your teeth into! Chapter 12 has eight easy crosswords. Chapter 13 has four medium crosswords and Chapter 14 has four hard cryptic crosswords. These difficulty levels are explained at the start of each chapter.

If you're keen to try more, check out the companion volume to this one, *Cryptic Crosswords For Dummies*, which contains a larger collection of cryptics written by me, with the same easy, medium and hard standards as I've used in this book.

Part 3: Hints and Answers

The part title gives it away, really. This part is a collection of helpful hints, and then, if you're really stuck, the answers.

Part 4: The Part of Tens

In this part I give you ten ways to improve your abilities as a cryptic crossword solver, helped by a review of ten (plus two!) of my favourite solving aids and reference tools.

This section of the book also contains an appendix, made up of a bunch of handy lists that you're going to need to refer to frequently on your cryptic crossword adventures.

Icons Used in This Book

As is standard with all *For Dummies* books, I'm using a set of icons to signpost a few special cases within each chapter. When you come across one of these icons, pay attention to the text next to it:

TIP

This marks a tip or a hint that you might find especially helpful when solving cryptic crosswords.

REMEMBER

This icon helps you to remember a few critical elements about cryptics.

WARNING

These warnings mark out places where getting tripped up is all too easy, as well as common areas of confusion.

Where to Go from Here

This book isn't intended to be read from front to back in order (although reading in this way gives you a nice 'course' in solving cryptics). If you're completely new to cryptics, I recommend you read Chapter 1 first. From there, each chapter in Part 1 delves into a particular cryptic clue device and includes a teaching crossword for that clue type, with each clue fully explained. So if you have some experience with cryptics and want to work on a particular kind of clue that's been deviling you, then turn to that chapter and be enlightened.

1

Diving Into the World of Cryptic Crosswords

In this part, we head straight into the mystifying world of cryptic crosswords! I provide you with some background to this form of brain puzzler, explain what makes a cryptic clue and reveal the tools of the trade. I also talk a little about how solving cryptic crosswords can help you stay sharp as a tack, no matter what your age!

After getting through the basics, most of the remaining chapters in this part delve into each of the major cryptic clue devices. One device is discussed per chapter, and each chapter contains sample clues and a mini teaching crossword that only uses that clue variety, so you can really hone your skills. I also show you how foreign words, names and abbreviations are used in clues.

At the end of this part, I go into more depth about cryptic crosswords around the world, explain the variations that exist in how clues are written and cover what makes a clue easy or hard.

Chapter **1**

Introducing Cryptic Crosswords

I n this chapter, I explain to you the absolute basics of crosswords in general and of cryptic crosswords in particular. I set out the common crossword terminology so you can find your way around the grid with ease, and reveal the anatomy of a cryptic clue (no clues were harmed in the process!). I list the main cryptic clue devices (which are all explained in detail in the subsequent chapters in Part 1), and tell you about indicator words. I even walk you through your first cryptic clue, step by step!

The basic equipment you need to do cryptic crosswords is listed, and I've included a rather handy checklist of my top tips for making a start on any crossword, as well as my top cryptic crossword solving tips. Solving cryptics also provides mental benefits, and I touch on these briefly.

Getting a Handle on Crossword Terminology

A few terms are good to know when discussing crosswords. I'll start with the absolute basics, in case you're not familiar with crosswords at all.

A crossword puzzle consists of a grid of black and white squares, some of which are numbered, and a set of clues placed near the grid. Crossword grids are usually an odd number of squares across and down — common grid sizes are 13 × 13 and 15 × 15.

Tiny *clue numbers* are placed in the corners of some of the squares, at the locations where a word starts. Once you've solved a clue, you write the answer into the grid, starting the word at the corresponding number on the grid. Answers can be entered either horizontally, called *across* entries, or vertically, called *down* entries.

So, for example, the answer to clue '8 across' is written into the grid, with the first letter going in at the white square with the tiny '8' in the corner, and the letters following subsequently across the grid. The clue numbers aren't used for anything else; they simply connect the clue and its answer to the correct position in the grid.

Starting at the corresponding clue number, as with across clues, down clues are written into the grid, from top to bottom.

The white squares of a grid are generally called just that — the *white squares*. The black squares can be called the *darks*, *blanks*, *blocks* or simply the *black squares*. In this book, I use the term *black squares*.

A white square that's part of both an across and a down word is said to be *checked*, *keyed* or *crossed*. A white square that's part of just one word is *unchecked*, *unkeyed* or *uncrossed* (makes a crazy sort of sense!). In this book, I use the terms *checked* and *unchecked*.

Figure 1-1 shows the basic elements of a crossword grid.

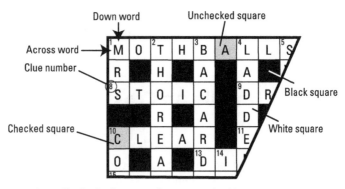

FIGURE 1-1: The basic elements of a crossword grid.

Some differences exist between the crossword styles popular in different countries. For example, American crossword grids are fully checked, with every white square in the grid being crossed by both an across and a down word. British grids have many more unchecked letters. (See the sidebar 'Looking at the difference between British- and American-style crosswords' for more on these different styles.)

The clues for a crossword are usually printed in two columns, one for the across clues and one for the down clues. In cryptics (and many British-style quick, non-cryptic crosswords), the *letter count* is in brackets at the end of the clue, which tells you how many letters are in the answer. Of course, you can discover this information for yourself by counting the relevant squares in the grid. However, the letter count also tells you whether a hyphen is present in the answer, or the answer's more than one word, which can be very helpful information. These quick clues illustrate these uses of the letter count:

Radiator additive **(4-6)** = ANTI-FREEZE

Decorative legume **(5,3)** = SWEET PEA

LOOKING AT THE DIFFERENCE BETWEEN BRITISH- AND AMERICAN-STYLE CROSSWORDS

The crossword was invented in 1913 by Arthur Wynne, a British journalist living in New York, and from there it evolved differently in the United States and the United Kingdom. This has led to various differences in these puzzles, depending on where you live.

In England and Commonwealth countries, two varieties of crossword exist: The *non-cryptic* or *quick* crossword, which has definition or synonym clues, and the *cryptic crossword*, which is devious and difficult (and the reason you're reading this book!).

(continued)

The words included in British-style crosswords, both quick and cryptic, tend to be 'normal' words, from a very wide (and occasionally archaic) vocabulary, proper names, the occasional foreign word and some abbreviations. In general, crossword setters try to avoid 'unpleasant' words in their grids — including names of lethal or severe diseases, sexual terms, gory words, swear words or racial slurs. These are thought to be poor form. Many British-style crosswords include a letter count at the end of the clue in brackets.

British-style crossword grids have a higher proportion of black to white squares than American grids. Quick crosswords have around 25 per cent black squares, and cryptic have around 35 per cent black squares. They are based on a sort of chequerboard pattern, with symmetrical grids. (The grid shown in Figure 1-1 is a British-style crossword grid.)

British-style crossword grids are seen worldwide, especially in Commonwealth countries such as Australia, Canada, New Zealand, India and South Africa.

In the United States, a nearly solid 'white' grid, with very few black squares, is most common. American crosswords often include brand names, abbreviations, slang, foreign words, sections of phrases, suffixes, prefixes and even word fragments. The grid structure dictates this sometimes odd assortment of letters — creating a completely overlapping grid of words is very hard, after all! The figure included with this sidebar shows a section of an American-style crossword grid.

American crosswords often have a theme and a title, which provides a clue to the theme. Generally the three to five theme entries are the longest words in the puzzle, and are placed symmetrically within the grid. American clues are quite varied, ranging from straight definitions to puns, quasi-cryptic clues and plenty of hard 'quiz' clues. While the straight definition clues are basically the same style as British quick (non-cryptic) crossword clues, the other varieties of clues often trip up those who aren't used to them! American clues don't have the letter count at the end — which generally makes the clue more difficult, because you don't get an indication of whether the answer contains more than one word, or whether it's hyphenated.

While a few newspapers in the United States do publish cryptic crosswords, they're rare. American cryptics also use the British-style grid, with a higher proportion of black squares. This has led to a misconception in America that only cryptics have this sort of grid.

Both American and British crosswords have sets of rules that setters have to follow: The grids need to be symmetrical, and one- and two-letter words aren't allowed. On top of this, many other clue-writing conventions also exist.

Neither the American nor British crossword is better or worse than the other; they're just different and both styles are challenging in their own ways. One thing to keep in mind when solving cryptics is that you don't need quite as many checked letters, because every cryptic clue provides two ways of finding the answer!

Understanding Clues and Discovering Answers

I know that cryptic clues look impenetrable when you first see them, and, to be honest, this is what the clue setter is trying to achieve!

When you first read a cryptic clue, the initial meaning seems very strange. This *surface meaning* is intended to mislead and distract you — but not permanently. The tussle between clue writer and clue solver is meant to be a friendly competition, but one that's always weighted in your favour. After all, the clue setter wants you to solve the crossword — eventually!

Your task is to see beyond the distracting surface meaning and look for the true meaning of each clue. A key factor in uncovering this true meaning is learning to read a clue word by word. This involves looking at every single word and assessing what each word might mean in the clue, one by one, rather than reading the clue as a little sentence or phrase.

As well as breaking the clue down into its individual words, some other general principles can be applied to most clues. In the following sections, I provide lots of tips on breaking clues down and getting started on working out answers.

Dissecting cryptic clues

Each cryptic clue is basically a very concise mini-puzzle. A cryptic clue contains a *definition* and a bit of *wordplay*. Yes, that's right. Cryptic clues contain the definition of the answer, in plain sight, such as you'd find in any quick, non-cryptic, crossword clue. However, cryptic clues also include other elements to point you in the right direction.

Finding the definition within the clue

The definition may be disguised somewhat, but, trust me, it's there! It usually resides at the start or end of the clue (not in the middle). A major key to cracking cryptics is to locate the definition within each clue.

REMEMBER

The definition part of a cryptic clue may not be an exact dictionary synonym for the answer — it may be a bit of a tangent away from that. It does have to be a fair definition, though, and has to match the part of speech of the answer (so a plural answer has to have a plural definition, for example).

The definition part of the clue may be similar to a regular non-cryptic crossword clue, such as *old vehicles* = TRAMS, or it may require a bit more of a stretch of the imagination, such as *they would be good for picnics* = SANDWICHES, which (while it's the definition section of a cryptic clue) isn't a dictionary definition for sandwiches.

Sometimes a definition in a cryptic clue presents you with an example of something and you need to extrapolate back from this example to the definition (these sorts of definitions are used in non-cryptic crosswords, too).

These sorts of clues often have *perhaps*, *for instance* or *for example* in the clue wording as well, and tend to work best where the answer is the name of a group of things. For example, BIG CAT could be defined in the clue as *lion, perhaps*, and MOUNTAIN could be defined as *Olympus, for example*.

At its most tangential, a river may be defined as a *flower* (it's something that *flows*, so therefore it's a *flow-er* — you may now groan!). So be prepared to look a little further afield for meanings or synonyms for the definition section of the clue, because the answer may not be the most obvious word that first comes to mind (and is likely to be more devious and obscure in harder cryptics).

The definition part of the clue may also suggest, say, a noun on the surface reading, but in fact be defining a verb. For example, *chip* in a clue may read initially as a noun meaning 'potato chip', but the setter is defining an answer that's actually a verb, meaning 'break off'.

Having fun with some wordplay

The wordplay part of the clue is (hopefully!) where the fun comes in. The setter may have used an anagram, reversed the letters or used some other device as another way of getting to the answer. You may also see the wordplay section of the clue referred to as the *subsidiary indication*, or just *subsidiary*, in various places.

Solving the wordplay side of the clue should give you the same answer as provided by the definition part of the clue. This means you get confirmation right away that you've got the right answer — something I love about cryptic clues. The wordplay and the definition should both lead to the same answer, and you get that satisfying 'Ah haaa!' moment.

TIP

Because each cryptic clue contains the definition and a bit of wordplay, once you've figured out which part of the clue is the wordplay element, the remainder of the clue can automatically be pinned down as the definition, and vice versa.

Roughly eight main types of wordplay devices are used in cryptic clues, as follows:

>> Anagrams (Chapter 2)

>> Charades, or linked words (Chapter 3)

>> Containers, or words inside other words (Chapter 4)

>> Subtractions (Chapter 5)

>> Reversals (Chapter 6)

>> Homophones (Chapter 7)

>> Double definitions (Chapter 8)

>> Hidden words (Chapter 9)

Looking out for indicator words

Along with the definition and some wordplay (refer to the preceding sections), many cryptic clues also include *indicator words*. These vital words are pointers to the sort of wordplay device involved, and give you some help on how best to solve the clue. For example, anagram indicators are words included in the clue like *stirred*, *mixed up*, *broken*, *cooked*, *muddled* and *confused* — words that indicate you need to alter the letter order of some of the words in the clue to get the answer.

TIP

Setters make the indicator words fit the clue. If they're writing a clue that has a surface meaning related to, say, motor racing, they choose indicator words that tie in with this theme — so an anagram indicator in such an automotive clue is likely to be something like *crashed*, *smashed up* or *broken down*, rather than *stirred* or *cooked*, for example.

REMEMBER

Setters try their best to disguise indicator words, and your task as the solver is to figure out the separate elements within a clue — that is, which words are the indicators, which are other parts of the wordplay and which are part of the definition.

Understanding linking words, punctuation and abbreviations

Even the small words and punctuation used in cryptic clues can be important — or an attempt to slow you down! Abbreviations are also widely used in cryptic clues, and are a common cause of confusion and frustration among new solvers.

Cryptic clues may have *linking words* in them, which help the clue to read well, and connect the definition and the wordplay to each other. These are generally short words (prepositions and conjunctions) and phrases such as *a*, *and*, *can be*, *causing*, *from*, *gets*, *has*, *in*, *is*, *provides*, *reveals*, *showing*, *with* and *yielding* (among many others). Not all clues have them, and setters and newspapers have different standards and preferences about their use, so depending on whose crosswords you're solving, you may come across these a lot, or not often at all.

Properly used, linking words should serve some function within the clue, usually giving a sense of equality (this equals that, so words such as *is*, *has* or *with* could be used), or showing that one part of the clue results in the other (with words such as *causes*, *yields* or *reveals* used).

Another thing to be aware of is punctuation in clues — it's generally there to confuse you, and make the superficial meaning read better. In general, it's safe to ignore it. You can also ignore any accents or other marks on letters. A question mark can sometimes indicate a need to think a bit more laterally, or indicate a particularly devious pun! And an apostrophe s ('s) may actually be an abbreviation of *is* or *has*. More on this in Chapter 2.

Cryptic setters often need to come up with ways of adding one or two letters to the wordplay. Rather than just saying 'Add an N' (that would be too easy, wouldn't it?!), they prefer to say 'Add an abbreviation for north'. Getting to grips with the hundreds of cryptic abbreviations is an essential part of learning to solve cryptic clues. Many abbreviations are obvious, and can be found in any dictionary (such as the chemical elements and common uses, such as *left* = L), but many are much less obvious (*excellent* = AI, because it looks like A1) or dated. I discuss abbreviations in more detail in Chapter 10.

REMEMBER

You may sometimes come across less common and harder sorts of grids and clues, particularly in British crosswords. These include barred grids, which have thick bars instead of black squares, and 'complete the obscure literary quotation' clues. I don't cover these rarer cryptic devices in detail in this book. If you really get into cryptics and want to take your solving to a higher level, I've provided a list of good resources for furthering your education in Chapter 18.

Putting it all together

Launching into a real cryptic clue can help you get a feel for the different elements within the clue. Take, for example, the following:

A headless brain drops (4)

On first reading, the setter (who me?!) is trying to make you imagine a squishy disembodied brain splatting onto the ground. This is the *surface meaning* — the first impression you get when reading a clue. Try to put this imagery out of your mind!

In this case, the definition is *drops*, and the wordplay is *headless brain*. The clue should be read as, 'A *brain* without its *head* (that is, its first letter) also means *drops*'. Another trick in this clue is that *drops*, which you might at first read as a verb (meaning 'falls'), is actually a noun, as in 'drops of water'. Can you see the answer? Yes, it's RAIN (BRAIN without B). That wasn't too bad, was it?

Getting started on the grid

As with most things in life, before you launch into solving cryptic crosswords, you should get yourself organised and do some planning.

Gathering your equipment

Before you tackle a cryptic crossword, gather your equipment (it won't take long!). The first thing you need is your brain — which is attached, so that one's easy.

Even the most experienced solvers make mistakes on cryptics, so a pencil and eraser are advisable.

TIP

I love using an erasable pen, because I find the darker ink easier to read than pencil, and it's still easy to correct errors. Plus you can look cool — 'Yeah, I do cryptics in ink!' — just don't reveal your secret!

Scrap paper is always handy. You need a place to work out anagrams and write down your ideas about clues.

You're likely to find some reference books very helpful — have a dictionary, thesaurus, crossword dictionary, and possibly a phrase book or two with the basics of languages like French, Italian, Spanish and German close at hand. Knowing the addresses of certain websites and online solving aids is also helpful.

TIP

Crossword dictionaries are particularly useful when solving cryptic crosswords. Apart from providing lists of synonyms, they include commonly used abbreviations, lists of cryptic indicators, foreign terms and lists of many other things (from constellations and rivers to characters from Shakespeare's works) sorted by letter length.

DISCOVERING THE HISTORY OF CROSSWORDS

Word grid puzzles have been around for thousands of years, but crosswords as we know them today are only about 100 years old. The first crossword was published in 1913 by Arthur Wynne, a British journalist living in New York. He was the chief editorial writer for the *New York World*, and part of his job was to come up with a page of puzzles for the Sunday edition of the paper. On 21 December 1913, he published his newest puzzle invention, entitled 'Word-Cross Puzzle'. It was a diamond-shaped grid, with a clear centre, without any black squares (so all the letters in all the words overlapped, or were checked). A few weeks later a typesetter at the newspaper made a mistake, and titled it a 'Cross-Word' — and this name has stuck ever since. Later on, Wynne added the black squares, and it started to look like the puzzle we all know today.

Wynne's new puzzle quickly became very popular in the United States, but it took nine years for it to cross the Atlantic and appear in the United Kingdom. This happened in 1922, in *Pearson's Magazine*. The first *Times* crossword (that bastion of difficult cryptic crosswords!) was printed in February 1930.

Crosswords became so wildly popular that in the 1920s they were even deemed to be a public menace! The craze for solving these puzzles led to dictionary damage in libraries, and made (according to the *Tamworth Herald*, in 1924) 'devastating inroads on the working hours of every rank of society'. Some libraries took to blacking out the crosswords in their newspapers to stop readers from hogging the papers. Crosswords were even blamed as 'the final blow to the art of conversation' and for breaking up homes — you have been warned!

Nowadays, finding a newspaper that doesn't include at least one crossword is rare. Thousands of websites are devoted to crosswords. Many newspapers and other providers are heading into the future with online puzzles that can be either printed out from a website or solved interactively on your computer or mobile device. Certainly, no sign exists of any reduction in the crossword's popularity!

These sorts of reference books and crossword dictionaries are especially useful when you're first learning about solving cryptics — before long, you won't need to rely on them quite as often. I discuss helpful websites, apps and books in Chapter 18, and provide lists of some abbreviations and other resources in the Appendix.

REMEMBER

I use resources such as dictionaries and phrase books when I'm *creating* cryptic crosswords, so I see no reason why you shouldn't use them in *solving* them. It certainly isn't cheating. The *minority* of solvers don't use references. Solving cryptics is an ongoing educational experience, and meant to be fun, after all. Unless you're actually in a cryptic crossword competition, where reference books are banned, go for it!

Planning your attack

So, you've got your brain, tools, reference books and websites to hand. What next? Here are my tips for making a start on any crossword, whether cryptic or quick:

>> Don't try to do the clues in order. The order you solve the clues in doesn't matter, and any answer you can put into the grid makes it easier for you to solve the words that cross over. Read through all the clues and see if any jump out at you as being something you think you can answer.

>> Draw a hyphen or bar on the grid when a clue's letter count shows the answer is hyphenated or more than one word (see Figure 1-2).

>> Check out the letter count, looking for shorter or very long words. Shorter words can be the easier words to guess, but so too can long words, because they have fewer possible solutions.

>> Look for clues where the answer looks like it may be a plural. Pencil in an S at the end of these clues. They may, of course, be an irregular plural (like MICE, FUNGI or DATA), but putting the S in might help.

>> If you have some checked letters (especially less common letters like K, Y, J, Z, V and W), see if you can just guess the word that goes into the space. If you have K_A_ _, for instance, a few options are KHAKI, KNACK, KNAVE, KOALA, KRAAL (an enclosure for stock or an enclosed village), KRAIT (a snake) and KRAUT (Sauerkraut).

>> If you're tackling a crossword online, use the 'hint' or 'cheat' function to reveal one or two of the longer words, which cross over the starting letters of other words. If solving a puzzle in a book, have a sneak peek at the answers, and pick out one or two long words to fill in. Having initial letters can really help.

>> If an answer you're pencilling in to the grid results in an awkward letter pattern in the crossing-over word, your answer may be wrong, sad to say. For example, not that many words start with X, V doesn't appear before S within words, and practically no words end with J. This sort of information can help you restrict the possible answers for a clue.

>> If you're very stuck on a clue, leave it for a while, even over-night. You may be surprised at what your subconscious can do. Often the answer suddenly seems completely obvious, after a break. And remember — this is supposed to be fun!

>> Crosswords in newspapers often get harder as the week goes on, so make a start with Monday and Tuesday puzzles, and avoid the weekend ones until you're more proficient.

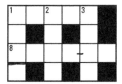

FIGURE 1-2: Mark on the grid where words are hyphenated (8 across) or the answer consists of two words (1 down).

TIP

Here's a list of tips specifically for solving cryptic crosswords:

>> The longest words in a cryptic crossword often use ana-grams in their clues.

>> The definition of the answer is in the clue, usually at the start or end of the clue. Locating the definition is an important step! Also keep in mind that the definition itself may be a little obscure, and not an obvious dictionary definition or exact synonym.

>> If you think you know what the answer may be (just from the definition), see if you can work backwards from it to figure out whether the wordplay section of the clue fits your answer.

>> Ignore the obvious 'surface' reading of the clue and instead look for the hidden meaning.

>> Look at each word in the clue one by one, rather than together as a sentence. Don't ignore a single word!

>> Ignore most punctuation, and all capital and accented letters in clues. Keep in mind that one or two words in the clue may lead to an abbreviation.

>> The definition has to match the part of speech and tense of the answer. So if the clue seems to be indicating a past tense verb, the answer should be a past tense verb as well. The same goes for plurals and so on.

>> Use a thesaurus to look for synonyms for words near the start or end of a clue — you can often stumble upon the answer this way and then figure out what the cryptic wordplay means after the fact. This is a perfectly acceptable strategy!

>> When you're first learning about cryptics, stick with one setter or series. Every setter writes clues slightly differently, and you're likely to be more successful if you get to know *one* setter's style and idiosyncrasies well, rather than trying a wide range of puzzles from lots of different newspapers and setters.

>> Practice and practice and practice. No book (no, not even this one) can enable you to instantly master this difficult puzzle genre. Solving cryptics takes practice. Practice daily if you really want to master them completely, and practice weekly if you're keen to be able to solve them well. As much as I'd love to have you grasp everything in this book rapidly, the reality is, if you're new to cryptic crosswords, there is a great deal to learn. With practice, and with the help of this book, you can improve — just don't expect it to be immediate.

Refer to the section 'Dissecting cryptic clues' for more on working through cryptic clues.

Benefiting from Crosswords

Despite initially having been blamed for most of society's ills (refer to the sidebar 'Discovering the history of crosswords' for more on this), crosswords in general are a fantastic way to improve your vocabulary, and cryptic crosswords in particular can improve much more than this. Solving cryptics uses your lateral-thinking skills, and develops your puzzle-solving skills. You need to look for alternative meanings beyond the surface meaning of the clues, think of all possible interpretations and meanings of each word in a clue, and become widely read in a host of areas.

While research has shown that physical exercise has many benefits — physical and mental — as you age, 'intellectual exercise' has been shown to be very valuable as well.

EYEWITNESSES AND CRYPTICS

In a fascinating piece of unusual research published in 2006, Dr Michael Lewis at the School of Psychology at Cardiff University studied the effects of reading and solving Sudoku, regular non-cryptic crosswords and cryptic crosswords on people who then were asked to identify faces in a staged identity parade. He was interested in seeing whether these 'time-filling' tasks (which are often done by people waiting to be called upon in these situations) would affect the accuracy of participants' performance.

In a very unexpected result, Lewis found that doing cryptic crosswords had a significant impact on the subjects' ability to carry out their facial recognition tasks, with much poorer results — while the other three activities didn't have this effect (and were roughly equal).

Lewis suggests that this may be something to do with the mental effort of suppressing the immediate and obvious meaning of the words in the clues, and that this 'suppression of the obvious' may also affect face recognition in the brain — however, exactly what's going on isn't clear. Some other tasks, such as describing an object a few minutes before doing the same identity parade tasks, also have a similar effect.

One lesson can be taken from this — if you're ever called upon to pick someone out in an identity parade, steer clear of the cryptics!

Some studies show that the risk of developing dementia, including Alzheimer's disease, may be reduced by such activities as solving crosswords, reading and playing card games. One important aspect that has been discovered about this sort of 'mental training' is that if you want to improve a particular function, such as your memory, you need to do activities that practice that skill, such as concentration and memory games. So, if you're keen to improve your lateral-thinking skills, vocabulary, general knowledge and reasoning, cryptic crosswords are the perfect medicine!

Chapter **2**

Untangling Anagrams

An anagram is a word or phrase formed from the letters of another word or phrase. So RATS, TARS and STAR are the anagrams of ARTS, for example.

Anagrams have been popular with people ever since they started writing language down — sometimes anagrams were even seen as a source of mystic power and magic. The word 'anagram' comes from an ancient Greek source — combining ANA (up or back) and GRAMMA (letter).

Many people derive a lot of fun from creating silly and apt anagrams, especially of politicians' names and suchlike: HE BUGS GORE is an anagram of GEORGE BUSH, MOON STARER is an anagram of ASTRONOMER and HERE COME DOTS is an apt anagram of THE MORSE CODE.

Anagrams are a device used in most cryptic crosswords, either as 'pure' anagram clues, where the entire answer is reached by jumbling up some other part of the clue, or as a part of a more complex clue, where a section of the answer uses jumbled letters. In this chapter, I cover all you need to know about how anagrams can be used within cryptic crossword clues — and once you've got a handle on anagrams, you can definitely make a good start on any cryptic crossword!

Mixing It Up with Anagrams

Anagrams in cryptic clues are anagrams of the answer word, and the letters to be jumbled up are in plain sight within the clue. Abbreviations (such as west = W) can also be used in anagrams, and these letters (generally just one or two) also need to be included in the anagram (see Chapter 10 for more information on abbreviations). You need to mix up these letters to get a new word that tallies with the definition or is a part of the answer.

The key to spotting an anagram is the *anagram indicator*. This is a word in the clue that tells you an anagram is present and you need to mix up the letters of a word (or two or three, and maybe an abbreviation) to discover another word. Anagram indicators are words that give a sense of something being broken, rearranged, stressed, upset, active, sick, confused, unusual, wrong, or even unattractive.

There are almost an infinite number of ways of indicating an anagram. Here's just a few anagram indicators: Arranged, awkward, bad, broken, changed, confused, cooked, crazy, distressed, drunk, excited, incorrect, jostling, kind of, loosely, mad, mangled, mistaken, mixed up, novel, odd, peculiar, stewed, stirred, tangled, ugly, upset, wriggly and zany.

TIP

Anagram clues are good examples of where the letter count, which tells you how many letters are in the answer, is helpful. As the letters to be rearranged to make the anagram are in plain view within the clue, look for a word or words in the clue that have the same number of letters.

Here's an example of an anagram clue:

Crazy gander is a risk (6)

While the surface meaning of the clue may make you think of running away from a deranged goose, the cryptic clue actually reads as, 'A *crazy* version of *gander* is a word that means *risk*'. The answer is DANGER, an anagram of *gander*. *Risk* is the definition and *crazy gander* is the wordplay. *Crazy* is the anagram indicator. See, it makes sense — honest, it does!

A rule followed in most cryptic crosswords is the letters used in the anagram must be in 'plain view' as a word in the clue (not a *synonym* of a word in the clue). So, a version of the clue above that says *Crazy **bird** is a risk* (6) isn't a fair clue. It's not reasonable to expect you to go through all the six-letter bird names (my *Chambers Word File* lists 103 of them) to find the one (*gander*) that's an anagram of a word that means *risk*. This sort of clue is called an *indirect anagram*, and is occasionally seen in very difficult cryptics.

Here's another example:

Eccentric master finds a creek (6)

While the surface meaning has hopefully created a nice mental image of a mad professor stumbling about in the bush searching for water, the clue actually reads as, 'An *eccentric* version of *master* (the only six letter word in the clue) *finds* a word that means *creek*'. The definition is *creek*, and the wordplay is *eccentric master*. *Eccentric* is the anagram indicator here and the 'fodder' to be jumbled up is *master*. The answer is STREAM.

Uncovering and Decoding Anagram Clues

When looking at any given cryptic clue, see if any words within it could indicate an anagram — for example, words that mean broken, confused, some sort of activity or movement, insanity, damage, rotation or even drunkenness may be anagram indicators. The main thing is that they suggest that the letters of nearby words, and maybe a letter or two from an abbreviation, in the clue need to be rearranged in some way.

WARNING

While anagram indicator words often highlight the existence of an anagram in a clue, they may also be a perfectly 'innocent' part of a totally different type of clue, such as the definition. Remember to think of *all* possibilities when working on clues!

If you see what you think might be an anagram indicator, look at the letter count at the end of the clue and see if any words (or combinations of words) in the clue add up to that many letters. Keep in mind that in some clues the anagram device is just used on a part of the answer, not all of it (in which case the letter count has limited value to you), and that abbreviations can be included in the anagrams.

Once you've found the anagram indicator, and think you know the letters to jumble up, you've also found the definition, which is the rest of the clue. Finding the definition is always your main goal!

If you can spot some likely anagram candidates, now's the time to use your pencil or pen and some scrap paper (refer to Chapter 1 for my recommendations about resources to keep nearby when solving cryptic crosswords). Write out the letters of the possible anagram in a random arrangement. See if you can rearrange them to form a new word, which is a synonym for what you think is the definition part of the clue. Easier said than done, I know, but not impossible!

Sometimes the words to be rearranged don't fall exactly next to each other in the clue, but might be linked with the words *and* or *with*, or similar.

Here are my tips on how to solve anagrams:

>> Write the letters of the word you're scrambling up backwards.

>> Write the letters in a circle.

>> Write the vowels in one group, and the consonants in another.

>> Look out for clues that have proper names in them — these are often anagram clues and the names are part of the anagram letters.

>> Check for words with dropped letters (such as *'e* instead of *he*) — these are often part of anagrams.

>> Try putting S at the end if the clue looks like it has a plural answer.

>> Look for common letter patterns such as TH, SH, HE, RE, ND, ED, ION, ENT and ING.

>> Watch out for common vowel–consonant combinations — for example, the consonant that most often follows a vowel is N (AN, EN, IN, ON, UN).

>> Look for common prefixes such as UN-, RE-, IN-, IM-, IR-, IL-, DIS-, DE-, MID-, AN-, AB- and EX- among the letters.

>> Try making common suffixes such as -TION, -AL, -ENT, -IVE, -ITY, -ER, -OUS, -FUL, -FY, -EN and -IC with the letters.

>> If you really get stuck, check out the great apps and websites available that can help you out of a tight spot. (See Chapter 18 for more on these.)

REMEMBER

When looking for possible anagrams and doing all your messing around with letters, always keep the definition in mind!

TIP

If you're working on a crossword and some of the crossing words have been filled in (well done!), mark these checked letters on your scrap paper. For example, you might have the pattern _R _ _S and the letters of *terse* to work with. Cross off the letters in *terse* that are in the grid already (R and S), and rearrange the remaining letters (TEE) within this pattern of blanks and letters. (TREES is the answer, by the way.)

The use of apostrophe s in a clue ('s) can be tricky in cryptic clues. While it reads as a possessive, it may actually be an abbreviation of *is*, and is roughly equivalent to an equals sign. An example:

Crushing a lemon's fruit (5) = MELON

This clue reads as, '*Crushing* the letters of *lemon* is/equals a *fruit*'. In this example, the *s* in *lemon's* isn't included in the anagram, but is actually part of the wordplay 'instructions'.

WARNING

While an apostrophe s may be the word *is* in disguise (and, therefore, not included in the letters to be jumbled up), this isn't always the case. It may be included — you just have to try both options!

Here are some more anagram clues, with the explanation following each clue — see if you can figure the clues out for yourself before reading their explanations and answers:

>> *Pastel hen confused huge animals* (9)

The anagram indicator in this case is *confused*. This clue is an example where more than one word forms the anagram — in this case, it's *pastel* + *hen* (which add up to the requisite nine letters). If you mix up these letters, you can work out the answer. *Huge animals* is the definition and it's a plural, so you can put the S at the end.

>> *Lamb's cries come from broken stable* (6)

The anagram indicator in this clue is *broken*. *Stable* has six letters and if you mix it up, you can find the answer, which means *lamb's cries*. Another plural clue, so try putting the S at the end. *Come from* are linking words.

» *Brad is agitated, dull, and boring* (4)

This clue illustrates one principle of cryptic clues — (mostly) ignore the punctuation. You can safely forget the commas in this clue. *Agitated* is the anagram indicator and *Brad* is the word to rearrange, or fodder. The answer means *dull and boring*.

» *Mad serpent has gift* (7)

Mad is the anagram indicator and *serpent* has the right number of letters to fit the answer. *Gift* is the definition. *Has* is a linking word.

The answers, in order, are ELEPHANTS, BLEATS, DRAB and PRESENT. How did you go?

So there it is — a basic introduction to anagram clues. Most cross-words have at least three or four of this sort of clue, and often more. Easier crosswords have a higher proportion of anagram clues, because they're usually relatively easy to spot and solve.

Anagram Crossword

Across

1. Beaten up, sore — all for a flower (4)

3. Incorrect laws lead to pointed tools (4)

7. Flying machine has cracked panel (5)

8. Unusually low bird (3)

9. Ineptly assuage the BBQ offering (7)

13. Feigned woe in debt (3)

14. The sea upset canoe (5)

16. Sheds were shut violently (4)

17. Confused pets move forward (4)

Down

1. Injured pore with cord (4)
2. Rotten sap comes from mineral spring (3)
4. Invalid grown in error (5)
5. Grain storage oils stirred up (4)
6. 'Suspense', he intones horribly (7)

10. Alter stew, wide awake (5)
11. High-class shop rearranged (4)
12. Damaged pans break suddenly (4)
15. Gobble up messy tea (3)

Clue explanations

Across

1. *Flower* is the definition and *beaten up* is the anagram indicator, working on *sore*. Ignore the punctuation.

3. *Incorrect* is the anagram indicator, affecting *laws*. *Pointed tools* is the definition.

7. *Flying machine* is the definition and *panel* is the anagram fodder. The anagram is indicated by *cracked*.

8. *Unusually* write *low* and you get a *bird*.

9. *Ineptly* is the anagram indicator, working on *assuage*. *BBQ offering* is the definition.

13. *In debt* is the definition, *feigned* is the anagram indicator and *woe* is the anagram of the answer.

14. Create an *upset* version of *canoe* and you find another word for *sea*.

16. *Violently* rearrange the letters of *shut* and you find another word for *sheds*.

17. *Confused* is the anagram indicator, *pets* is the word to scramble up and *move forward* is the definition.

Down

1. *Pore* is the anagram, indicated by *injured*. *Cord* is the definition.

2. *Rotten* is the anagram indicator, working on *sap*. *Mineral spring* is the definition.

4. Write *grown* in an *invalid* way (*invalid* here isn't a sick person!), to get a word meaning *in error*. It can be a bit tricky, I admit, to spot which words are the anagram indicators in this clue, because *in error* could also be the anagram indicator, with a definition of *invalid*! In this case, just try both options, to see which one works out.

5. Write *oils* in a *stirred up* way, to get a word that means *grain storage*.

6. Remember to ignore the punctuation. *Suspense* is the definition — you can find the answer by writing *intones* in a *horrible* way. *He* is just there to help the clue read better.

10. *Stew* is the anagram indicator, *alter* is the word to — well — alter, and *wide awake* is the definition.

11. *High-class* is the definition, the answer can be found by *rearranging* the letters of *shop*.

12. *Break suddenly* is the definition part of the clue, *damaged* is the anagram indicator and *pans* is what to work on.

15. Make a *mess* of the letters of *tea* to find a word that means *gobble up*.

Crossword answer

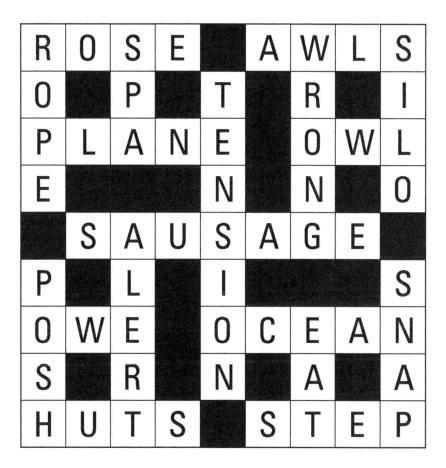

Chapter **3**

Charade Clues: Piecing Together Linked Words

Linked words, or *charades*, are a very common device used in cryptic clues. Every cryptic crossword has many of these clues, either as 'pure' charade clues, or in combination with other clue devices.

So, what are they? You know the game 'Charades', where the audience has to guess the word, title or phrase, through someone miming the answer bit by bit? Well, charade clues run along the same principles: You're given the hints for each part of the answer, bit by bit and (generally) in order. If the parts aren't in order, you're given instructions on which bit comes first and which bit comes next.

As an example, CATERPILLAR could be clued as a charade of CAT + ER + PILLAR. CAT and PILLAR are easy to write synonyms for, but the ER is more tricky. Abbreviations are often used in charades. In this instance, the ER could be clued as *hesitation* or *queen* (from Elizabetha Regina).

In this chapter, I run through everything you need to know about charade clues and give you an opportunity to put your new knowledge into practice, using a sample crossword.

Playing Charades

As with most cryptic clues, clues using linked words or charades have a definition and some wordplay. Your goal is to figure out which part of the clue is which, and then solve the wordplay and find the answer.

Linked word clues are, however, a bit unusual in that they don't always have a cryptic indicator that tells you what sort of clue you're looking at. In general, indicator words aren't needed, because the words in the clue occur in the same order as they do in the answer, one after the other, and the only device (which isn't really a 'device') is finding synonyms, abbreviations or definitions for the words in the wordplay section. If indicators are used, they are there to help make the clue read better or highlight instances where the components aren't in order.

So, what you've basically got with the charade device is

(Definition for a word) + (Definition for another word) = (Definition of the answer)

Abbreviations are very commonly used in charade clues, to clue a few letters.

Sometimes small words in a charade are just left as is, in plain view, and you don't have to work out a synonym for them (these words are usually short and common words). In which case your 'clue equation' is

(Definition for a word) + a word = (Definition of the answer)

So, let's try out an actual charade clue:

Ocean boy's spice (6)

In this clue, the definition is *spice*. It's not yet clear whether *spice* is a noun or a verb here. All you do to solve this sort of clue is come up with one-word definitions, abbreviations or synonyms for the words in the wordplay part of the clue. So, in this instance, you need synonyms for *ocean* and *boy*. How about SEA and SON?

When you put them together, in order (SEA + SON), you end up with SEASON, another word for the (verb) *spice*! The apostrophe s is just telling you that one part of the clue (ocean boy) is the same as the other part (spice).

For some of the examples in this chapter, I'm giving you the definition right away, but this won't be clear when you're solving a clue by yourself. To get started, look at the start and end of each clue for the possible definitions. You mostly need to try several possibilities before hitting on the correct interpretation of the clue.

Locating the definition in a clue is a very important part of solving it!

Here's another example of a charade clue that uses this 'one-word-after-another' formulation:

Worker runs off to get married with fast animals (9)

Worker/s, in cryptic clues, often refers to social insects — ant/s and bee/s are the favourite choices. In this case, ANT is the word we're after. *Runs off to get married* is another way of saying ELOPES. So we have ANT + ELOPES = ANTELOPES, which are *fast animals*! *With* is a linking word.

Another example:

Meaning in canvas (6)

This clue reads as, 'Another word for *meaning* is *in* + a synonym for *canvas* (TENT)'. The answer in this case is IN + TENT = INTENT. Note that *in* is in plain sight and no synonym is required for it.

And one more:

Irish emblem is a fake stone (8)

In this clue, the definition is at the start again (*Irish emblem*) and the wordplay is *fake stone*. SHAM is another word for *fake* and ROCK is another word for *stone*. This gives us SHAM + ROCK = SHAMROCK.

Clue setters commonly have to find a way of indicating a single letter or pair of letters in many sorts of clues, including charades — and they have come up with hundreds of ways of doing so. Lists of these abbreviations are often seen in crossword dictionaries; here are just a few examples:

>> *North, south, east* and *west* in clues often indicate the letters N, S, E and W respectively.

>> *Left* is L, *right* is R.

>> Roman numerals are often used so if a clue mentions a number, think of these (*five* = V, *ten* = X, *hundred* = C, *thousand* = M and so on).

>> Simple words in other languages are often used, such as *the* in French (LA, LE, LES), German (DAS, DIE, DER), Spanish (EL, LA) or Italian (IL, LO, LA, LE).

>> Musical terms are sometimes used, especially *piano (soft)* = P and *forte (loud)* = F. Singing voices are also used: *Soprano* = S, *alto* = A and so on.

>> Chemical element symbols are sometimes used (for example, *gold* = *AU*) — so dust off your periodic table!

>> The phonetic alphabet is popular: *Alpha* = A, *bravo* = B, *Charlie* = C, *echo* = E, *Lima* = L, *sierra* = S, *tango* = T and so on.

>> Many words are abbreviated in funny ways, or make use of standard abbreviations: *Able seaman, tar* or *sailor* = AB; *no good* = NG; *first person* = I; *vitamin* = A, B, C, D or E; *kiss* = X; *that is* = IE; *Connecticut* = CT; *quiet* or *hush* = SH; *extraterrestrial* = ET; *bachelor* = BA (that is, Bachelor of Arts) and so on (ad infinitum?!).

I talk about how abbreviations are clued in more detail in Chapter 10, and a list of the more common abbreviations appears in the Appendix.

Here's an example of a charade clue that uses an abbreviation:

Worker takes tenor a red vegetable (4)

That worker's here again! This time it's a *bee*. It *takes* the letter T (*tenor*), giving you BEE + T = BEET (*a red vegetable*). *Takes* is a bit of a charade indicator here, telling you that one word takes on or adds on to another.

And another example:

Tether the French tree (5)

The definition is *tether*, and the wordplay is *the French tree*. The clue reads as, '*Tether* is also *the* (in French) + a *tree*'. You don't need to know the French word for tree; *the* (in) *French* is the part to figure out (LE, LA and LES are your choices). LE is the correct one here, which leaves three letters to figure out in the answer.

Now we need the name for a type of tree that's only three letters long. With a little trial and error, you can discover that LE + ASH fits the bill, giving LEASH (or a *tether*) as the answer.

Picking Out and Solving Charade Clues

Charades are a widespread cryptic device, and you'll find a lot of these clues in any cryptic crossword. Sometimes a charade is all that's used in a clue, and sometimes it may be a part of a longer clue that uses an anagram or some other device as well.

Some charade clues use indicators, although in general they aren't necessary. If you spot words that give a sense of adding one thing to another thing or putting things next to each other, they may indicate a charade clue. Examples of charade indicators include *added to*, *and*, *before*, *by*, *following*, *joining*, *next to*, *on*, *over*, *plus*, *takes* and *with*.

Occasionally, the word sections are put out of order, depending on how the clue setter has written the clue. In these situations, the clue must tell you which bit goes where — so you may see indicators such as *after*, *first*, *second* and *finally*.

In these instances, the direction the answer has in the crossword grid can make a difference to the wording of the clue. An across word might have words such as *left, right, behind, in front of, before, after, east* or *west* in it. A down clue might have words such as *on top of, under, above, below, north* or *south*.

These 'direction' indicators can be rather tricky to spot, because all kinds of words that mean *behind, before, in front of* and so on can also be used in other clue devices. However, only down clues can use *on top of, under, beneath* and so on, because of how they're written into the crossword grid.

Here's an example of a down clue:

Highland gold is under the dish (7)

This clue also uses one of the cryptic abbreviations covered in the section 'Playing Charades', earlier in this chapter. The clue reads as, 'A synonym for *highland* is *gold* (AU) put *under* or after *dish* (PLATE)'. So you have PLATE + AU = PLATEAU.

REMEMBER

Not all the words in a cryptic clue are synonyms or abbreviations — sometimes the letters to use are right there in front of you! This is usually the case with shorter common words such as ON, AS, IF, AT, OR, IT, HE, SHE, THE, OF and IS.

Here's an example where some of the letters for the answer are already provided in the clue:

Humanist at robbery (7)

This clue reads as, 'A synonym for *humanist* is *at* plus a synonym for *robbery* (HEIST)'. So the answer is AT + HEIST = ATHEIST.

And another example:

A smart outfit, or a boyfriend? (6)

This clue reads as, 'A synonym for *boyfriend* is another word for *a smart outfit* (SUIT) + *or*. And ignore the comma and question mark!' This gives you SUIT + OR = SUITOR.

WARNING

Don't always ignore question marks — they can sometimes indicate a pun, that you need to read the clue in an even more lateral way (it's possible!), or that only the surface meaning of the clue is a question.

REMEMBER

A well-written charade clue shouldn't split a compound word into its 'logical' parts — such as AIRPORT clued as a synonym for AIR + a synonym for PORT, or SANDPAPER clued as a synonym for SAND + synonym for PAPER. However, this style of clueing is sometimes seen.

TIP

Here's a list of tips for spotting and solving charade clues:

>> This is a widely used cryptic device, and most crosswords have a high proportion of these clues.

>> If a clue doesn't seem to have any cryptic indicator words, keep in mind it could well be a charade clue.

>> A charade may be part of a longer clue, so keep an eye out for them in all sorts of cryptic clues.

>> Be on the lookout for clues that have linking words that indicate one word is added to another (such as *and*, *with*, *after* and *plus*).

>> Look for prepositions that indicate words being put *after*, *above*, *behind*, *before* or *under* other words.

>> Look for synonyms and abbreviations for all the words in the clue and check if any of them fit together to form another word.

>> Remember that sometimes short words in the clue are included in the charade as is, in 'plain view'.

>> Look for words that might indicate an abbreviation. Remember that an abbreviation is part of the wordplay, so spotting one can help you to pin down the definition as well (provided in the other part of the clue).

The charade device pops up in many other cryptic clues as well, so other sample crosswords in this book also use this device!

Charades Crossword

Note: Creating tiny crosswords that only have words that can be clued by simple charades is difficult! This grid isn't fair, according to normal construction rules, so I've put in a few extra letters to give you a helping hand. These clues do include abbreviations. Check the Appendix if you need a list to refer to!

Across

1. Left card in netting (4)

3. Loud and ancient layer (4)

6. Soft, fuming sulphur for brigands (7)

9. Held back sailor, blemished (9)

12. Short hopper gets potassium at the castle (4)

13. Self-satisfied soprano has a large cup (4)

14. Vitamin study leads to great fear (5)

Down

2. Greek letter from Charlie — Hello! (3)

4. On eastern unit (3)

5. Yes! German dish for an island nation (5)

7. Motor decay reveals a vegetable (6)

8. Proverbs notice grows old (6)

10. Southern chilly rebuke (5)

11. Wanderer is no lunatic (5)

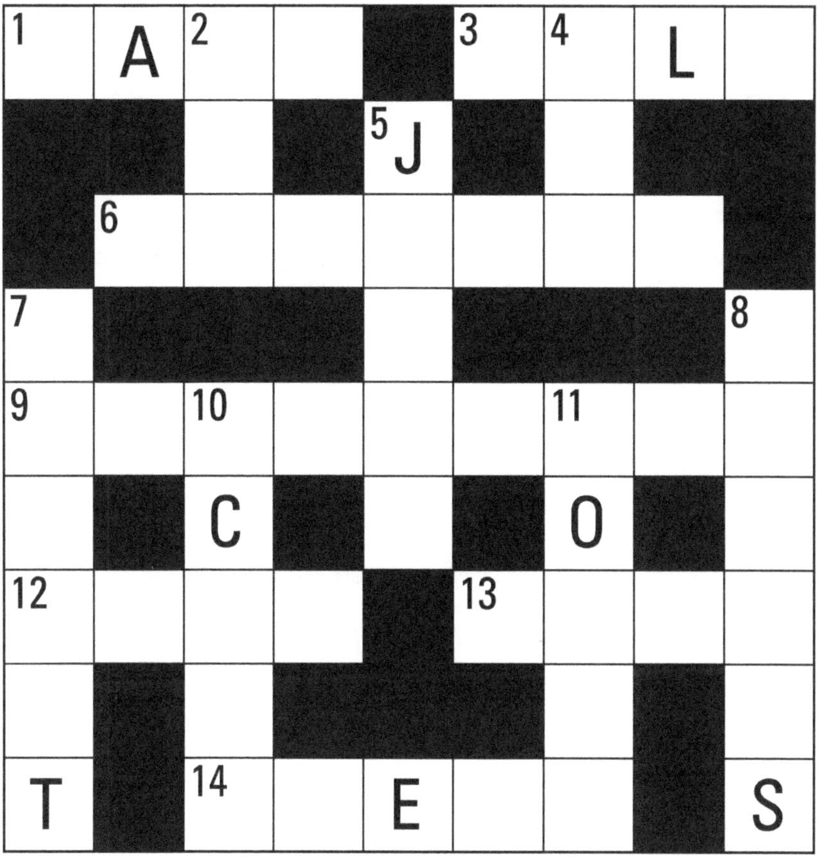

Clue explanations

Across

1. *Left* is abbreviated to L and *card* can be an ACE. *Netting* is the definition.

3. *Layer* is the definition. *Loud* is an abbreviation for F (as in forte, in music) and *ancient* is also OLD.

6. This clue has three parts in the charade. *Soft* = P (as in soft or quiet music), *fuming* = IRATE and *sulphur* = S. *Brigands* is the definition.

9. *Held back* is the definition. Sailor = AB (which stands for able seaman) + STAINED is another word for *blemished*.

12. A kangaroo hops, so a *hopper* is a (rather tangential) synonym for KANGAROO. It's also *short*, so abbreviated to ROO. Add on K (*potassium*). *Castle* (as in the chess piece) is the definition.

13. *Self-satisfied* is the definition. S is an abbreviation for *soprano* — add on MUG (*a large cup*).

14. The definition is *great fear*. *Vitamin* can indicate A, B, C, D or E (D, in this case). READ is another word for *study*, which you put after the *vitamin* (D).

Down

2. *Greek letter* is the definition. The answer can be made from *Charlie* (C, from the phonetic alphabet) added to *hello* (HI).

4. *On* is read as is (ON) and *eastern* = E. *Unit* is the definition.

5. German *yes* is JA and a *dish* is a PAN. *Island nation* is the definition. Remember to ignore the punctuation!

7. *Motor* = CAR, *decay* = ROT. The definition is *vegetable*.

8. *Proverbs* is the definition. A *notice* is an AD and add on *grows old* (AGES).

10. *Southern* is an abbreviation for S; *chilly* also means COLD. *Rebuke* is the definition.

11. *Wanderer* is the definition. This can be discovered from NO (*no*, in plain view) + MAD (*lunatic*).

Crossword answer

L	A	C	E			F	O	L	D
		H		J		N			
	P	I	R	A	T	E	S		
C				P					A
A	B	S	T	A	I	N	E	D	
R		C		N		O			A
R	O	O	K		S	M	U	G	
O		L				A			E
T		D	R	E	A	D			S

Chapter 4
Putting Words Inside Words

A device often used in cryptic clues is the *container clue*, where one word acts as a container for another word, and these two (or three) words go together to provide the answer. They can also be clued as one word being around, or outside of, another (so they're sometimes called *contents and container clues*).

In this chapter, I break down container clues, help you learn to spot them and provide a sample crossword that uses this type of clue.

Comprehending Containers

So what does a container clue look like? Well, here's a little example:

Noble knight's boy is in agony (7)

In this clue, the apostrophe s actually means *is*, rather than showing possession. So the clue reads *noble knight* is also a synonym for *boy* (LAD) put *in* another word for *agony* (PAIN). Giving us PA(LAD)IN.

And another one:

We surrounded the strike, Snowy (5)

Snowy is the definition in this clue. Ignore the punctuation and capital letter of *Snowy*! *Surrounded* is the container indicator. So, surround a synonym for *strike* (HIT) with the letters of WE (no synonym required), and you come up with the answer: W(HIT)E.

As you can see from these two examples, containers can be used in a couple of ways — either a word or some letters are put inside another word or a word is surrounded by another word or letters. In the first variety, the container indicators are words that mean 'putting inside'. In the second variety, the container indicator words have the meaning of 'surrounding' something.

The container device is often used in longer cryptic clues, so you may see it in combination with other cryptic devices such as anagrams, reversals and deletions.

Detecting and Decoding Container Clues

To spot a container in the cryptic clues you're trying to crack, the first thing to do is look for any indicator words that have the sense of 'putting in' or 'wrapping around'. The lists included in this section show a sample of the many possible words that can be used in this role.

Container indicators, where one word is put *into* another, include the following:

» Contained by
» Filling
» Holds
» In
» Included
» Inside
» Involved in

- >> Kept in
- >> Ring
- >> Trapped in

Container indicators, where one word is put *around* another, include the following:

- >> About
- >> Around
- >> Caught
- >> Circling
- >> Embracing
- >> Grasping
- >> Hugging
- >> Outside
- >> Taking in
- >> Wearing
- >> Without

WARNING

Without is sometimes used as a cryptic indicator and, because it's a bit of a special case, it can create problems. Most of the time, *without* as a cryptic indicator means 'lacking' (that is, remove a letter or two). But, very occasionally, it's used as a container indicator, with the more obscure literary meaning of 'outside' (as the opposite of within).

REMEMBER

A cryptic clue has a definition and a wordplay section — and figuring out the definition is a vital part of cracking the clue! Each section of the clue should give you the same answer. Once you've identified the container indicator and the words to work on, the part of the clue that's left is the definition.

It doesn't matter if the answer is a hyphenated word or has more than one word — just ignore the hyphen and spaces between words for the purposes of finding the answer. For example:

Change around mother's past school (4,5)

Another word for *change* is ALTER. Put the letters from ALTER around another word for *mother* (MAMA). The definition is *past school* and ALMA MATER is the answer — you can see that the MAMA is split between the two words of the clue (AL**MA MA**TER), as is ALTER, but this doesn't matter.

On reading this clue, thinking that *change around* is an anagram indicator is quite reasonable — but this isn't the case! As you can see, sometimes the words in clues are cryptic indicators and sometimes they aren't — no wonder they're confusing!

TIP

In the preceding example, you can see that the answer is nine letters long. If it were an anagram clue, the letters to be scrambled up have to be there in plain view in the clue. None of the words (that aren't indicator words), in any combination, adds up to the requisite nine letters (*mother, past, school*), so this can help you to eliminate the anagram device from consideration.

Abbreviations are used a lot in container clues, so be on the lookout for the various ways that cryptic setters 'encode' one or two letters. I provide a brief list of some of these in Chapter 3, and they are discussed in much more detail in Chapter 10. A longer list of abbreviations is in the Appendix.

Here's an example of a clue that encodes a single letter required for the answer:

Creek's vapour gets around castle (6)

This clue read as, 'A synonym for *creek* is another word for *vapour* put *around castle*'. So *creek* is the definition, *gets around* is the container indicator, *vapour* is a synonym for STEAM, and *castle* is abbreviated to R (for rook, chess notation). All this gives you STREAM! Phew!

As with all varieties of cryptic clues, the container device can be used in conjunction with other devices, especially in more complex cryptic crosswords.

Container Crossword

Note: Because I've created a small crossword with as many container clues as possible, this teaching grid doesn't adhere to the usual standards for cryptic crosswords — an adequate number of checked squares isn't provided, for starters. I've put in some extra letters to help you get started.

Across

1. Rodents outside steal from bacterium (7)

5. Receive around about welcome (5)

7. Italian capital — one thousand buried in fish eggs (4)

8. A long way off, circling eastern terror (4)

10. Aching, embraced west, and cursed (5)

11. Plant seeds around large room, it's trivial (7)

Down

2. Violin string put in Ruby Marsh Grass (4)

3. Put her potassium in juniper spirit, to make pickle (7)

4. Fizzy candy gelled around culinary plant (7)

5. Pastimes put me in fumes (5)

6. Sewn edge inside note subject (5)

9. Intent lass takes in a duck (4)

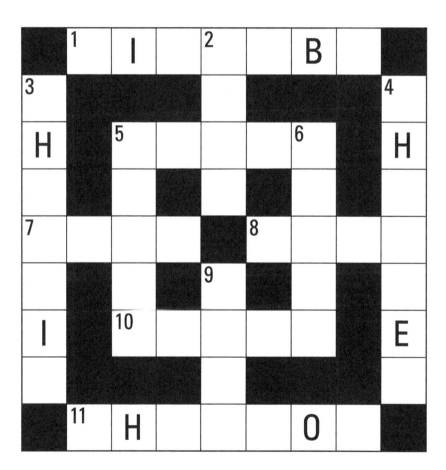

Clue explanations

Across

1. MICE are *rodents*. Put them *outside* ROB (*steal from*), and you discover a *bacterium*!

5. GET is another word for *receive*; put it *around* RE, which is an abbreviation for *about*. The definition is *welcome* (5).

7. *Italian capital* is the definition. The answer is the Roman numeral for *one thousand* (M) *buried* in *fish eggs* (ROE).

8. *Terror* is the definition and it's the same as *a long way off* (FAR) *circling* (container indicator) E (abbreviation of *eastern*).

10. *Cursed* is the definition here. The letters of SORE (*aching*) *embraced* (went around) W (abbreviation for *west*).

11. *Plant seeds* is another way of saying SOW. Put these letters *around* a synonym for a *large room*. *It's* is a linking word and *trivial* is the definition.

Down

2. *Violin string* is an abbreviation for E (E, A, D and G are the options here), which is put in RED (*ruby*) to create another word for a type of *marsh grass* (4). Ignore those capital letters!

3. In this clue, *her* just equals HER! *Potassium* is abbreviated to K (its chemical symbol). Both of these are put in GIN (*juniper spirit*) to make a *pickle* (the definition).

4. *Fizzy candy* is the definition here. SET is *gelled* and it goes *around* HERB (*culinary plant*).

5. The definition is *pastimes*. The wordplay is to *put* ME *in* GAS (*fumes*).

6. A *sewn edge* is also a HEM. Put it *inside* an abbreviation for *note*. In cryptic crossword-ese, *note* often refers to musical notes, and the Sol-Fa system in particular. You may recall the 'Do-Re-Mi' song from *The Sound of Music*? In this clue, *note* = TE. *Subject* is the definition.

9. *Intent* (as a noun, not an adjective!) is the definition. GAL is a *lass* and she *takes in* (container indicator) a *duck*, which is O. This last abbreviation may need some explanation! This is a cricket abbreviation, which is often seen in cryptics. In cricket, a batter's score of no runs is called a duck, or 0 (zero runs). In the crazy world of cryptics, turning a number that *looks* like a letter into that letter is quite acceptable — so 0 = O.

Crossword answer

IN THIS CHAPTER

» Discovering how to remove letters from words in cryptic clues

» Substituting letters in clues

» Trying out these clues for yourself in a practice crossword

Chapter **5**
Using Subtraction

Despite the wide variety of cryptic devices that setters have up their devious sleeves, most of the time words in the crossword grid don't fall easily into one of the tidy cryptic patterns (such as a reversal, covered in Chapter 6, or anagram, Chapter 2).

In such circumstances, setters may be able to clue the answer with a deletion or subtraction — they start with a longer word, tell you which letters to lop off it and, voila, you have the answer. For example, the word HANK could be clued as THANK without the T.

In this chapter, I cover recognising and solving clues that use subtraction and provide a sample crossword that uses this device.

Deleting Letters

Cryptic clues often have an indicator word or two (or more, sometimes) in them, which tells you what to do with the wordplay section of the clue to get to the answer.

Deletion indicators are words that (not surprisingly) indicate that something has been cut out of or off from the word. Some general deletion indicators are words like *abandoned*, *cut*, *dropping out*, *has no*, *lacking*, *left out*, *less*, *losing*, *not featuring*, *omitting*, *out* and *short*.

If the first letter needs to be removed, the deletion indicator might be a word or phrase like *decapitated*, *headless*, *leader absent*, *losing head* or *topless*. The first letter can also be indicated with words such as *at first*, *beginner*, *capital*, *entrance*, *initial*, *opening* or *top*. Here's an example of this sort of clue:

Assault, chopping the top off plait (4)

In this clue, *chopping the top off* is the deletion indicator. Another word for a *plait* is a BRAID. Remove the first letter and you get a word that also means *assault* (RAID). See, it makes perfect sense!

If the last letter is removed, the deletion indicator may be something like *almost*, *curtailed*, *cut short*, *reduced*, *tailless* or *take a bit off*. The last letter can also be indicated with words such as *at last*, *conclusion*, *ending*, *final*, *lastly*, *tail* or *ultimately*. Here's an example of this sort of subtraction:

Inferno cut short jacket (5)

This clue reads as a *jacket* (BLAZER) *cut short* (deletion indicator) also means *inferno* (BLAZE).

And if the middle letter of the word needs to be removed, the deletion indicator can run along the lines of *heartless*, *gutless* or *without heart/core/centre*. Here's another example, this time with a middle letter removed:

Heartlessly mount stockings (4)

A *mount* is also a HORSE. Looked at *heartlessly*, we take out the heart, or middle letter, of the word (R). This leaves us with HOSE, another word **for** *stockings*. Ta dah!

Needing to delete one or two letters anywhere in a word is also fairly common — in these cases, the letters to be deleted may not be the first, middle or final letters. The letters to be deleted are usually indicated with an abbreviation (see Chapter 10), or may be 'in the open' (especially if it's a very short word like A, AM, IT or I, for example). Other cryptic devices can be used in combination with these deletions, too. Here's an example of this sort of clue:

Thunderbolt blew off hard foot covering (4)

In this clue, a *thunderbolt* is a SHOCK (and nothing to do with the weather!). *Blew off* is the deletion indicator and *hard* leads you to H (think of pencil leads). SHOCK minus H = SOCK, which is a *foot covering*.

Sometimes, more than one letter is removed from the start or end of a word, and the deletion indicator should reflect this. Plural words such as *heads, early stages, tails, final parts* or *ends* (along with the words that indicate subtraction) would work in these cases. If more than one middle letter needs to be removed, these letters must be the exact middle letters (with an equal number of letters left on either side). If both the first letter and last letter are to be removed, the indicator word is something like *endlessly, missing covers* or *without edges*.

Another special case is when half of a word is cut off. In this case, the deletion must be exactly half of the word, and either the first half or the second half (not a scattered bunch of letters). Indicators for this sort of deletion are phrases such as *half gone, not half* and *half off*. An example of this sort of wanton destruction of a word — all in the (tragic!) pursuit of finding an answer — is as follows:

Blue fish tank is 50% off (4)

Half off is the deletion indicator here. What's *50%* or *half off*? The *fish tank* (AQUARIUM). Cutting AQUARIUM in half gives you AQUA + RIUM. Hopefully, deciding which half to use to get the answer for the definition *blue* is obvious!

Swapping Letters

There is one clue device that works along the same lines as a subtraction clue (refer to the preceding section) but, as well as one letter being deleted, the deleted letter is then replaced with another one. These are called *substitution* clues. Typically, you start with one word, swap one letter from it for another letter and end up with the answer. For example, if you take BIND and delete the N and replace it with R, you get a BIRD. These sorts of clues are indicated with words such as *for* (one letter *for* another), *in place of, instead of, replaced with, rather than* and so on. The letters to be deleted are usually indicated with abbreviations (for more information on common abbreviations see Chapter 10 and the Appendix).

Here's a simple example of one of these sorts of clues:

Baked treat using Fahrenheit instead of Celsius? It isn't genuine (4)

A CAKE is a *baked treat*. Use F (*Fahrenheit*) *instead of* the C (*Celsius*), to arrive at FAKE, which *isn't genuine*!

Solving Subtraction Clues

Because of their nature (lopping letters off left, right and centre, quite literally), subtraction clues often have short answers. A 'pure' subtraction clue isn't very likely to clue one of the longest words in a cryptic crossword.

Skim through the set of clues in the crossword and look for indicator words that may be pointing to the subtraction or substitution device. Keep in mind that subtractions can be used as part of a longer, more complex cryptic clue, such as part of a container clue (refer to Chapter 4) or an anagram (Chapter 2). A subtraction mostly refers to a single letter being deleted, but can also refer to a couple of letters or half of a word.

REMEMBER

The synonym you're looking for from the wordplay section of the clue is longer than the answer, usually by one letter. So if the letter count is (5), for example, the synonym for the wordplay part of the clue is likely to be six (or maybe seven) letters long.

Sometimes the word to be curtailed appears in the clue in plain sight (and you won't need to find a synonym). For example, the letter pair DR (or RY) might be clued as *almost dry*. In other words, it's *almost* the word DRY, but not quite!

Look for what the wordplay is telling you to do — you might need to swap one letter for another, for example.

Subtraction Crossword

Across

2. Single sailor left shellfish (5)

4. Feast cut short, producing loud noise (3)

5. Drink addition trimmed grain (3)

6. Carry tribal emblem with end lopped off (4)

8. Condensed miniature shopping centre (4)

10. Travel, with time for river's coastal rise (4)

14. Fruit crop up without early stages (4)

16. Vehicle from half of job (3)

17. Swamp missing Mr Cinders (3)

18. Cave-dwelling monster rambles endlessly (5)

Down

1. Hate leader missing from rostrum (5)
2. Relatives without uranium produce workers (4)
3. Short craft cereal (3)
4. Bargain sticker lost centre (4)
7. Coda in vogue, without an effort (3)
9. File headless viper (3)
11. Almost tweak measurement (4)
12. White wader has no initial remorse (5)
13. Vocal stony ocean dweller has no entrance (4)
15. Therefore, lost right sense of self (3)

Clue explanations

Across

2. The deletion indicator is *left*. Here it refers to the letters AB (*sailor*, from able-bodied seaman) being removed *from* another word for *shellfish* (ABALONE), for a five-letter word that also means *single*.

4. In this clue, seeing which parts are the wordplay (the first section) and which part is the definition is (hopefully) quite easy. The linking word *producing* helps here. A synonym for *feast* is DINE. If DINE is *cut short*, you get another word that means *loud noise*.

5. *Drink addition* is the definition here. RICE is a *grain* and *trimmed* is the deletion indicator.

6. *Carry* is the definition in this clue. I'm sure you can tell that *lopped off* is the deletion indicator, working on *tribal emblem* (TOTEM).

8. *Shopping centre* is the definition and you need another word for *miniature* (SMALL). Then, it needs to be *condensed* !

10. This is a substitution clue, indicated by the words *with* X *for* Y. In this instance get another word for *travel* (RIDE), put in a T (*time*) for, or instead of, R (*river*), to get a word that also means *coastal rise*.

14. *Without early stages* is the deletion indicator and, because it's plural, more than one letter needs to be cut off another word for *crop up* (APPEAR). How many letters to remove isn't always clear, but it's usually just two or three. *Fruit* is the definition.

16. *Vehicle* is the definition here. This is another less common deletion indicator — *half*. Another word for the adjective *job* is CAREER and you need half of it.

17. Another word for *swamp* is MARSH. *Missing* is the deletion indicator. In this clue, *Mr* just refers to those letters — MR. So subtract MR from MARSH, and you get a word that also means *cinders*. Pay no attention to those capital letters.

18. *Rambles* is another way to say STROLLS. Look at STROLLS *endlessly* — you need to delete both ends of the word. You discover a *cave-dwelling monster* this way!

Down

1. *Leader missing* is a deletion indicator, telling you that the *leader*, or first letter, is absent from a synonym for *rostrum* (PODIUM). This reveals another word for *hate*, which is the definition.

2. *Relatives* in this case are AUNTS. *Without* is the deletion indicator and *uranium* leads to the letter U (the chemical symbol). So remove U from AUNTS, and you get some *workers* (a common cryptic definition for social insects).

3. *Cereal* is the definition here. It can also be found in another word for *craft* (BOAT), *short*.

4. *Bargain* is the definition. A DECAL is a *sticker*. The deletion indicator is *lost centre* — you know what to do!

7. *In vogue, without an effort* is the wordplay portion of this clue (and, therefore, *coda* is the definition). *Without* is the deletion indicator. This clue is a bit harder. Rather than just lopping off the start or finish of the word, you need to come up with a whole word to delete — a synonym for *an effort* (TRY). Remove these letters from a synonym for *in vogue* (TRENDY) to get the answer.

9. *File* is also RASP. *Headless* is the deletion indicator and *viper* is the definition. Easy!

11. *Almost* is the deletion indicator here — it's telling you that the word is *almost* all there, but not quite! PINCH is another word for *tweak* and *measurement* is the definition.

12. *White wader* is the definition. *Has no initial* is the deletion indicator, telling you to remove the *initial* (or first) letter from another word for *remorse* (REGRET).

13. *Has no entrance* is the deletion indicator in this clue. So you need to remove the first letter from a synonym for *stony ocean dweller* (CORAL). You need to find another word for *vocal* (the definition).

15. *Therefore* is also written as ERGO and it has *lost right* (abbreviated as R). If you delete the letter R from ERGO, you discover another word that means *sense of self*.

Crossword answer

O				A	L	O	N	E
D		D	I	N		A		
I	C	E		T	O	T	E	
U		A		S			N	
M	A	L	L		T	I	D	E
	S			O		N		G
	P	E	A	R		C	A	R
	G		A	S	H			E
T	R	O	L	L				T

Chapter **6**
Examining Reversals

The English language is quite an extraordinary thing. It's so diverse, having been built from bits of many languages — all of which have different typical letter patterns (just think of the French words BOUQUET and CLICHÉ, German words SCHNAPPS and GESTALT, and Japanese words HAIKU and TYCOON). Because of the wide range of letter patterns seen in English, sometimes words form different words when read backwards.

BAT becomes a TAB, when read back to front. RAIL becomes a LIAR. DENIM is MINED. These sorts of two-way words are called *anadromes*, and roughly 900 of them exist in everyday English.

I'm sure you know about *palindromes* — those words that read exactly the same when read backwards. The list of these words is understandably much shorter than the list of anadromes. A few examples are TOT, BIB, GIG, PUP, PEEP, NOON, REFER, STATS and (aptly) ROTATOR.

Reversals are a popular cryptic device. Occasionally, a whole word can be reversed and form part of a tidy 'pure' reversal clue. More often, though, a reversal applies to only part of a word — for example, FREED could be clued as F + DEER going backwards.

In this chapter, I run through reversal cryptic clues, and then provide a sample crossword using this type of device.

Going Backwards with Reversals

Cryptic clues have a definition (which may be a bit tangential, but should be a synonym for the answer) and wordplay. The type of wordplay is revealed to you using an indicator word or two. (Refer to Chapter 1 for more on these basic elements of cryptic clues.)

In reversal clues, the indicator words (as you might expect) give a sense of something being turned around or over, going backwards or being reflected. Some examples are *backing up, flipped over, going back, knocked over, rejected, reversed, returning, the other way, the wrong way* and *turned over.* These sorts of indicators can be used for either across or down clues.

If the word is a down word, 'vertical reversal' indicators may be used. These are words such as *climbing, going north, going uphill, rise, sent up, skyward, turned up* and *upset.*

If a palindrome is used in a clue (which is rare), you may see indicators that highlight the word reads the same *in either direction,* or is *unaffected when overturned,* for example.

Here's an example of a 'pure' reversal cryptic clue:

Hay growths come back (5)

The reversal indicator here is *come back.* The word to work on is *growths* (the indicator word/s should be sitting next to the rest of the wordplay). Another word for *growths* is WARTS. If you read it backwards, you get STRAW (or *hay*). You can be sure that *hay* is the definition, because you've identified the wordplay section of the clue as *growths come back,* so all that's left is the definition!

As with some other cryptic clues (homophone clues in particular — see Chapter 7), if the reversal indicator is in the *middle* of a clue, they can be a bit confusing, because which part of the clue is the wordplay isn't clear. In these cases, look for checked letters in the grid to help pin down the answer. Here's an example of this sort of ambiguous reversal clue:

Issue reversed spell (4)

I'm sure you can spot the reversal indicator here — it's *reversed*. Because it's in the middle of the clue, being sure whether it's working on the *spell* end of the clue or the *issue* part is difficult. The clue reads as another word for *issue* (EMIT) being *reversed* to reveal a word that also means *spell* (TIME). If this clue was in a crossword, you can use the intersecting letters to resolve any ambiguity.

Noticing and Decoding Reversal Clues

TIP

When tackling a cryptic crossword, here are some tips on what to do to spot reversal clues:

>> Most 'pure' reversal clues are for short words — four or five letters is typical, so look closely at clues for these shorter words.

>> Read each clue in the crossword, keeping an eye out for any words that give a sense of something running in reverse, up, backwards or in the opposite direction. These may be reversal indicators.

>> Reversals are often used as a part of a longer cryptic clue — so, for example, they may be part of a charade clue or a container clue.

>> Palindrome clues are rare, but fun when they do occur! Look for indicator words that give the impression of the answer reading the same in either direction.

>> Down clues can have reversal indicators that give a sense of vertical movement, such as *reading from bottom to top*, *climbing up* or *going north*.

Reversals Crossword

Across

1. Condemned contrarily, to fulfil promise (7)
5. Exist for retiring age (3)
6. Cooking vessels wind up knocked over (4)
9. Returning separates the leather cord (5)
12. Current wild dog travels west (4)
13. It's a sheep, no matter how you look at it (3)
14. Pudding sent back, it has hair! (7)

Down

2. Climbing seat to get sacks (5)
3. Raised glass container to British rule in India (3)
4. Refunded nappy in lift (6)
7. Shoots back part of letter (5)
8. Uplifting prize for sliding box (6)
10. Sailing ship going north to ponds (5)
11. Return five two times to get a mesh (3)

Crossword grid:

| ¹D | | 2 | | V | | 3 | | 4 |
| 5 |
6			7			
⁸D						A
	9				10	
A					D
	11		12			
13
	14		E			D

Clue explanations

Across

1. *Fulfil promise* is the definition. *Contrarily* is the reversal indicator and *condemned* (REVILED) is what to reverse. How did you go?

5. *Retiring* is the reversal indicator. Working out the parts of the clue may be a bit tricky because the reversal indicator's in the middle of the clue, so whether it's working on *exist* or *age* isn't too clear. *Exist* is the definition here. *Age* is also ERA.

6. *Cooking vessels* is the definition. *Wind up* (STOP) gets *knocked over*.

9. *Returning* is the reversal indicator. PARTS (verb) is another word for *separates*. This leaves *leather cord* as the definition.

12. *Current* is the definition here. The reversal indicator is *travels west*. A WOLF is a sort of *wild dog*. (If you didn't know what sort of clue this was already, you could have read this as an anagram clue, because *wild* can be an anagram indicator!)

13. This is a rare palindrome clue! No matter which direction you read this word from, the answer is still a word that also means *sheep*.

14. *It has hair* is the definition here (*it has* are not linking words!). *Sent back* is the reversal indicator, and DESSERT is also the UK mass noun *pudding*.

Down

2. *Climbing* is the reversal indicator (appropriate for a down clue) and a synonym for *seat* (STOOL) is what to reverse. *To get* is a linking word. *Sacks* is the definition here (and a verb, not a noun).

3. *British rule in India* is the definition in this clue. *Raised* is the reversal indicator and *glass container* (JAR) is what to reverse.

4. You spotted the reversal indicator right away, didn't you? Yes, it's *in lift*. Because this indicator's at the end of the clue, it's clearly 'acting on' a synonym for *nappy* (DIAPER). Because it's all that's left, *refunded* must be the definition.

7. *Back* is the reversal indicator here but, because it's in the middle of the clue, which part of the clue it's working on is unclear. Try both options and see which answer fits into the grid! But because I'm nice (honest), I can tell you that *shoots* also means FIRES and *part of letter* is the definition.

8. A *prize* is also a REWARD. *Uplifting* is the reversal indicator and *sliding box* is the definition.

10. A sailing ship (SLOOP) is *going north* (an appropriate down clue reversal indicator) to get *to* a word that also means *ponds*.

11. *Return* is the reversal indicator, working on *five two times* (TEN). The definition is *mesh*.

Crossword answer

Chapter **7**

Decoding Homophones

One of the fascinating things about English is that a whole bunch of English words sound the same but are spelled differently and have different meanings. I know this 'feature' may be seen as confusing (or plain old annoying) to many people (especially those learning English as a second language), but it's great in cryptic crosswords!

Homophones is the fancy grammar term for these words that sound alike (*homo-* meaning 'same' + *-phone* meaning 'sound'), but have different meanings and spellings. Pairs such as BERRY/BURY, THROWN/THRONE, TWO/TO and SORE/SAW are all homophones — along with hundreds more (no wonder English is so baffling!).

In this chapter, I cut through the confusion and cover how homophones can be used in cryptics, and then give you a chance to work through a sample crossword that only uses homophone clues.

Saying Homophones Aloud

A very particular type of cryptic device uses homophones, and this device is usually quite easy to spot. Because they're so easy to find, usually no more than two or three of these sorts of clues appear in a cryptic crossword, and sometimes none appears (especially if none of the words in the grid lends itself to homophones). If you can find a homophone clue in a list of cryptic clues, however, this is a good place to start!

The homophone indicator words are all words that give you the instruction to listen to the sounds of the words or say a part of the clue aloud. This is because these clues are describing two words that sound alike.

The cryptic indicators you may come across include *announced, audibly, broadcast, declared, I hear, in conversation, on the air, on the radio, overheard, rumoured, said, sounds like, so to speak, talk about, uttered* and *vocally*.

One of the reasons homophone clues are easy to spot is that these particular indicator words aren't also used to identify other cryptic devices, unlike many other indicators. (Yes, *overturned*, I'm looking at you! *Overturned* can indicate both an anagram and a reversal.) Of course, what looks like a homophone indicator may turn out to be some other part of the clue; however, in general, it's a safe bet that if words in a clue give the sense of something being said or listened to, it's almost definitely a homophone.

Here's an example of a homophone clue:

It sounds like powder for blossom (6)

In this clue, *it sounds like* is the homophone indicator. The word to 'work on' is *powder* (FLOUR). The definition part of the clue is *blossom* (a synonym which *sounds like* FLOUR). The solution is FLOWER. See, that wasn't so bad!

One convention followed by most cryptic setters, most of the time, is that the homophone indicator is immediately before or after the word you need to find a synonym for (which sounds like the answer but is spelled differently). However, if the indicator is in the middle of the clue, which part of the clue the indicator's operating on isn't clear (a bit like the reversal clues, covered in Chapter 6).

The letter count can help here. If, for example, the clue leads you to the homophone pair MISSED and MIST and the letter count for the answer is given as (4), you can be sure that MIST is the answer to write into the crossword grid and not MISSED, which has six letters.

If the homophone pair has the same number of letters, like SWEET and SUITE, and you're not sure which one belongs in the grid, look for checked letters from crossing over words in the grid to give you further clues.

REMEMBER

In general, homophones are the only device used in a clue, but very occasionally you see them combined with other cryptic devices (such as an anagram) to make a clue work.

Homophones are also sometimes used to clue one or two letters in isolation, as part of a more complex clue. Some of these abbreviations are likely to be all too familiar to those used to text messaging. A few examples include the following:

>> Are = R
>> Bee = B
>> Cue/queue = Q
>> Ewe/you = U
>> Eye = I
>> Owe = O
>> See = C
>> Tea = T
>> You = U
>> You are =UR

When these 'single letter' homophones are used, they ought to have a homophone indicator — so you know you need to listen to the sound of the word to come up with the letter. (However, not all setters follow this convention.)

Sometimes regional dialects are used in homophone clues — most notably Cockney, which is generally seen in harder British cryptics. Rhyming slang may be used (for example, *trouble* and *strife* = WIFE) or the classic 'dropped H' (for example, *Cockney hair* = AIR).

Some harder versions of homophone clues may also be used — for example, *indirect* homophone clues, where the meaning of the homophone gives a 'sub-definition' to some words in the clue. This is then used to get to the final solution. But don't worry — none of the sample crosswords in this book uses indirect homophones or relies on your knowledge of Cockney slang. I don't want to scare you off!

Spotting and Solving Homophone Clues

Never forget — your goal with every cryptic clue is to locate the definition part of the clue. In some cryptic crosswords, no homophone clues appear, and in some only a couple are used — and generally no more than three.

When you read a clue and see a word or phrase that gives you the sense of listening to something or speaking something aloud, you've probably found a homophone clue. The homophone indicator is generally sitting next to the word to be 'worked upon'.

You then find a synonym for this word — this synonym sounds the same as the answer for the definition section of the clue. The letter count can help you to figure out which of the two homophones is the answer to write into the grid.

If you're really stuck as to which of the two options is the correct answer, and they have the same letter count, work on other entries in the grid to come up with some crossing-over checked letters.

Here's an example to illustrate homophone clues:

Music group is prohibited on air (4)

In this clue, *music group* is the definition. *On air* is the homophone indicator, so you need to come up with a synonym for *prohibited* (BANNED) and say it aloud to get the answer. I'm sure you don't need me to tell you the solution!

Another example is the following:

Storyteller played instrument loudly (4)

Storyteller is the definition — *loudly* is the homophone indicator — and it sounds the same as a *played instrument* (an instrument that is played) said aloud. The answer's only short — in this instance, it's LYRE.

And one more:

Knitted stitch sounds like a gem! (4)

In this clue, *knitted stitch* is the definition. *Sounds like* is the homophone indicator and *gem* is the synonym to 'speak aloud' (PEARL). This clue is a bit more tricky, because the homophone indicator is in the middle of the clue instead of at either end so, in theory, it could apply to either the first part of the clue (*knitted stitch*) or the last part (*a gem*). This is an instance where the letter count really helps — the answer has four letters (and not the five seen in PEARL). PURL is the answer (of course!).

Homophone Crossword

Note: Because only a relatively small number of words can be used to create a homophone-only crossword, I've had to break the usual grid design symmetry conventions, just this once! Some extra letters have been added to the grid to help you along the way.

Across

1. Talk about alloy for courage (6)

4. By the sound of it, dried fruit is present (7)

6. According to rumour, an Egyptian goddess gives frozen treats (4)

8. Securing roof, it's announced (7)

10. Infuses a contusion, audibly (5)

Down

1. European noble comes from large tent, I hear (7)

2. We hear crew swarm (4)

3. Dog's feet reportedly take a break (4)

4. Take bites noisily (6)

5. Poisons sound alarm bells (7)

7. Outspoken, conceited blade (4)

9. I heard latest antelope (3)

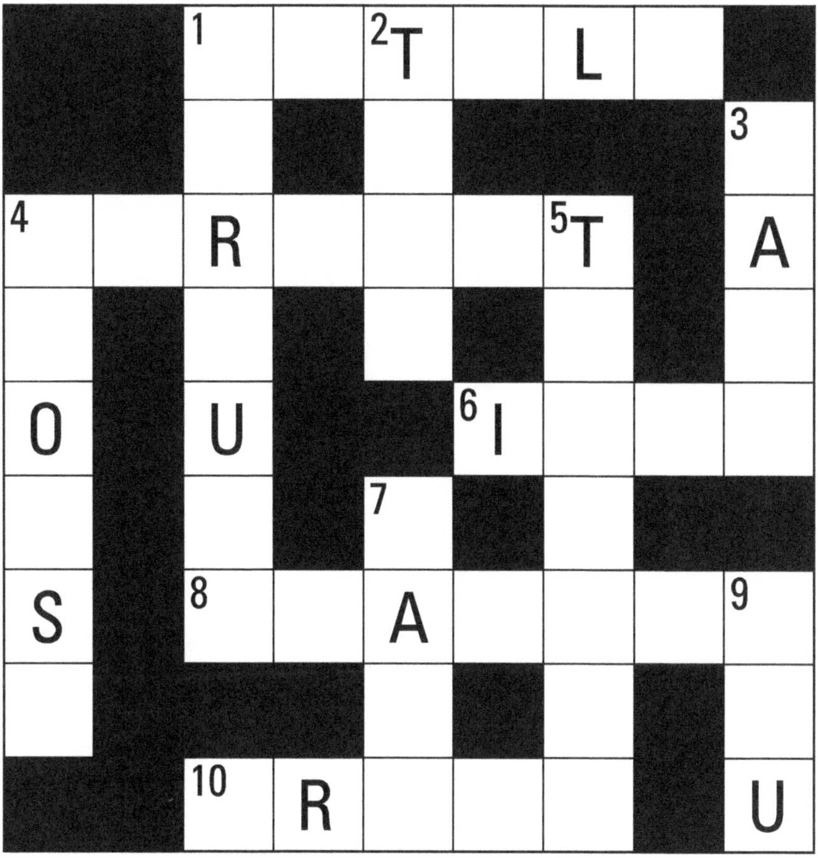

Clue explanations

Across

1. *Talk about* is the homophone indicator. Another word for *alloy* is METAL. *Courage* is the definition and the answer has six letters.

4. The homophone indicator is at the start of this clue, too — *by the sound of it*. Say a synonym for *dried fruit* (CURRANT). The definition is *present*, as an adjective.

6. *According to rumour* is the homophone indicator. The word to say aloud is right next to it — *an Egyptian goddess* (ISIS, that darling of crossword setters everywhere). Her name *gives* the definition, *frozen treats*.

8. In this clue, *securing* is the definition. *It's announced* is the homophone indicator and you need to say a synonym for *roof* aloud (how about CEILING?).

10. *Audibly* is the homophone indicator. What can you hear? A synonym for *contusion* (BRUISE). Now that you know the wordplay part of the clue, it's clear that *infuses* has to be the definition. Ignore that comma!

Down

1. *European noble* is the definition of this clue. The answer *comes from* saying another word for *large tent* (MARQUEE). *I hear* is the homophone indicator, but you already knew that, didn't you?!

Note: This clue illustrates an occasional complication with homophone clues — how words are pronounced. The answer to this one (MARQUIS) has a couple of correct pronunciations, and if I wasn't able to explain it to you, I probably wouldn't use this word with a homophone clue in a crossword.

The same problem can arise in areas with strong local dialects, because one word may be pronounced quite differently. A homophone clue may not work if the reader's accent is different from the setter's accent!

2. *We hear* is the homophone indicator here. *Crew* is next to it, so it's the word to say aloud (well, a synonym of *crew*, anyway — how about TEAM?). *Swarm* is the definition.

3. *Dog's feet* is the definition (it's a plural, too, so you can pencil in an S at the end!). *Reportedly* is the homophone indicator and *take a break* are the words to find a synonym for and then say aloud (PAUSE). Because the homophone indicator is in the middle of the clue, either *dog's feet* or *take a break* being the definition is possible — this is another instance where the letter count helps you. PAUSE has five letters, while PAWS has four (which matches the clue letter count).

4. *Noisily* is the homophone indicator (I bet you didn't need me to tell you that by now!), and the word sitting immediately next to it is *bites*, so that's the word to find a synonym for and say aloud (CHEWS). *Take* is the definition.

5. This is another clue where the homophone indicator (*sound*) is in the middle, so whether you need to work on *poisons* or *alarm bells* may be confusing. The letter count helps here. *Poisons* are also TOXINS (six letters) and *alarm bells* are also TOCSINS (seven letters, which matches the clue information), so *alarm bells* is the definition here.

7. *Outspoken* is the homophone indicator (you're getting the hang of this now!), *conceited* (VAIN) is what to say aloud and it also means *blade*, which is the definition.

9. *I heard* is the homophone indicator, *latest* is the word to say aloud (NEW). Since you've located the wordplay component of this clue, you can now deduce that *antelope* is the definition.

Crossword answer

Chapter **8**

Interpreting Double Definitions

D ouble definition clues are just what their name suggests — two definitions for the same word, written one after the other. That's it.

Cryptic crossword clues run along the same lines for most clues — that is, definition = wordplay, possibly with an indicator word or two = answer. (If you need to find out more about these basics, check out Chapter 1.) Double definition clues take this construction one step further. Using the preceding equation, they are definition = wordplay, which is *another* definition = answer.

In this chapter, I cover how double definition clues are used, give you some pointers on recognising them within cryptic crosswords and provide a sample crossword that uses this type of clue.

Delving into Double Definitions

As you're aware, no doubt, a vast number of words in English have more than one meaning. Sometimes these different meanings can be different parts of speech, such as a noun and a verb. (I think SET wins the prize — I counted 138 definitions for SET in the *Shorter Oxford English Dictionary*!) Sometimes a single word can even have noun, verb and adjective definitions — think of BABY, which can mean an *infant* (noun), *to pamper someone* (verb) and *immature* (adjective). This multiplicity of definitions is exploited in double definition clues.

Here's an example of a double definition clue:

Spoils red planet (4)

This is simply two definitions for MARS, strung one after the other — Mars as noun, the fourth planet in the solar system, and mars as a verb, meaning 'impairs the quality of'.

Setters do, of course, try to make these clues as tricky as they can and, despite double definition clues consisting of two 'straight' definitions strung one after the other, they can still be quite challenging to spot and solve. You may often find yourself totally stuck on a cryptic clue, trying all the tricks you know to crack it — anagrams, containers, abbreviations, reversals, the whole nine yards — when suddenly the penny drops. It's a double definition! At this point, you slap your forehead and write in the answer (or is that just me?).

Setters sometimes use *heteronyms* — words that are spelled identically but have different meanings and *different* pronunciations. Here's one: DOVE (the bird, pronounced 'duv') and DOVE (plunged down, pronounced 'doh-v'). Say these words aloud — see how they sound different? That's a heteronym. Here's another one: PRESENT (a gift) and PRESENT (hand over). Often, a slight difference exists in vowel sounds, and/or which syllables are stressed.

Because heteronyms are still spelled identically, they're deemed to be fair game for use in double definition clues (and, in fact, heteronyms were how double definition clues got started in the first place, all those years ago).

Sometimes the setter uses a very rare or archaic definition for a word as one of the definitions, and this can lead you astray. For example, while you probably know that BOLT can be a large metal pin, a flash of lightning, crossbow arrow, to run away suddenly and even a roll of fabric, you probably don't know that it's also a verb meaning to pass powder through a sieve. So a setter might write a clue such as the following:

Sieve flour and run away (4)

Chances are, on first reading of this clue, you wouldn't immediately think that BOLT was the answer.

The *and* in the preceding clue is important. While indicator words aren't required in these sorts of clues, some linking words sometimes act as double definition indicators.

Linking words in double definition clues can give the impression of the two definitions or parts of the clue:

>> Being produced from each other (*makes, provides, gives, shows, from, that, by*)

>> Belonging together (*of, having*)

>> Contradicting each other (*but, or, though*); this comes from the one word having two completely different, and probably contradictory, meanings

>> Existing together (*with, when, in which*)

>> Linking together (*and, to, for, with, as, so*)

Punctuation is sometimes used in double definition clues as indicators, so this is one of the few cases where you do want to pay attention to punctuation and see whether it's indicating a double definition clue. The marks used are

>> A comma (,) or a dash (—) to separate the two definitions

>> Apostrophe s ('s) to indicate belonging of one definition to the other

And the last trick that's sometimes used with these clues is the use of *coined words* (sometimes called 'language abuse'!). These are words which — while formed from standard parts of English (prefixes, suffixes and words) — are created by the setter and given a new meaning. Although the use of coined words is fairly rare, some setters do rely on them more heavily.

For example, DESIGN can be defined in a cryptic clue as DE-SIGN (*remove a signature*). DEVICE can mean DE-VICE (clued as *cast out wickedness*, perhaps?). Here's an example clue, using DEVICE as defined previously:

Apparatus to cast out wickedness? (6)

Apparatus is the first (and proper) definition for DEVICE. Then you have the coined meaning, DE-VICE, quirkily defined as *to cast out wickedness*. They both lead you to the one word to put into the crossword grid. The question mark alerts you that the use of a word or some words in the clue isn't normal.

Those special cryptic words such as FLOWER = river (a thing that flows), SHOWER = someone who shows something, and TOWER = someone who tows something, are also examples of this sort of language abuse. A TITLED woman could point to a woman's name that makes up a well-known book title (REBECCA or EMMA, perhaps?). BOOKED can have the same warped meaning: Something that's seen on or in a book. And a candle is WICKED (it has a WICK, get it?). Groan . . .

Definitions that include language abuse may appear in any sort of cryptic clue, not just in double definitions. You've been warned!

Here's a double definition clue example to try:

Sick person is not legally recognised (7)

The *is* helps a bit here and points the way to one half of the clue being the same as the other half of the clue. The first definition in this clue is *sick person* and the answer to this part also means *not legally recognised*. The answer is INVALID. These words are heteronyms, with different pronunciations.

Here's another example:

Hold on to castle tower (4)

This clue has no linking words — it's just two definitions, one after the other (although it's possible to think the *to* might be a linking word). Have a go at inserting an imaginary comma between the groups of words: *Hold, on to castle tower*? This doesn't offer much help. *Castle tower* rather sounds like one definition, and putting the comma before *castle* gives you your two definitions: *Hold on to* and *castle tower*. KEEP is the answer, of course.

Identifying and Decoding Double Definition Clues

Here are some tips for searching out double definition clues:

>> When reading a clue through, mentally put a comma in between the various parts of the clue, to see if separating the parts in this way suddenly makes a double definition clue obvious. This 'mental comma' is just a way of dividing up the clue, breaking up the surface meaning and testing whether a double definition is there in front of you.

>> If you see any letter pairs in words in the clue that might be prefixes, such as DE-, EX-, RE- and so on, or could be suffixes, such as -ER or -ED, see if the words they're on can break down into a coined word. This sort of 'language abuse' should be indicated by a question mark.

>> Short clues may be double definitions.

>> If you can't spot any obvious indicator words, you may be looking at a double definition clue.

>> Use a dictionary or thesaurus to check the definitions of the words in the clue and see if they match up. Especially look for obscure definitions!

>> Remember that practice makes perfect, and don't be discouraged if you often miss these sorts of clues. They *are* hard to spot, and even the best solvers miss them. They are also hard to solve, because none of the usual wordplay help is offered!

Double Definition Crossword

Note: This sample grid is a little non-standard, so I've put in some extra letters to help you out.

Across

1. Move along slowly a small distance (4)

3. Decoy put ornamental harness on horse (4)

6. Complain and fish (4)

7. Blonde's honest (4)

9. Travel by air to annoying insect (3)

12. Bewitches with ways in (9)

13. Wrench despicable fool (4)

14. Zero affection (4)

Down

1. Inflame joss stick (7)

2. Smoke meat to restore to health (4)

4. Bring up hind part (4)

5. Repeats mindlessly 'Bright birds' (7)

8. Don't sink cash for expenses (5)

10. Leading lady with celestial body (4)

11. Greek nymph's reflection (4)

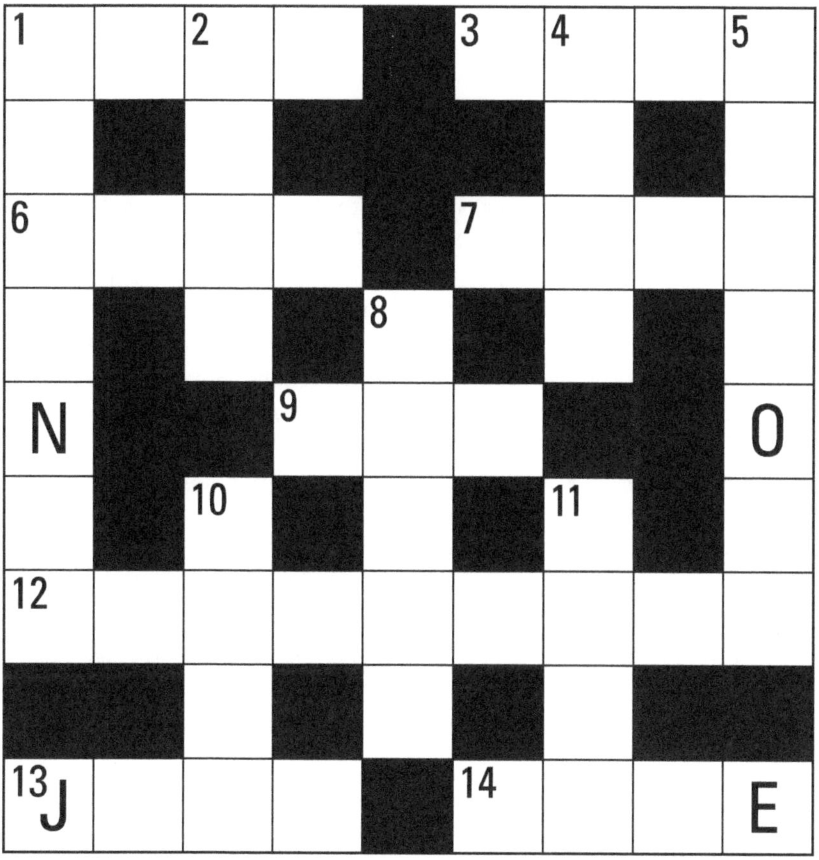
1
2
3
4
5
6
7
8
N
9
O
10
11
12
13 J
14
E

Clue explanations

Across

1. *Move along slowly* is the first definition and *a small distance* is the second definition. The answer starts with I.

3. This clue uses an archaic definition. *Decoy* is the first definition, and *put ornamental harness on horse* is the archaic second definition. The answer starts with T.

6. In this clue *and* is a linking word, which can indicate that a double definition clue is in play. The clue is basically saying that the answer can be defined as a synonym for *complain, and* as a synonym for a *fish*. The answer starts with C.

7. The apostrophe s (*blonde's*) can be expanded to say the answer is a synonym for *blonde*, which *is* also defined as a synonym for *honest*. The answer starts with F — I'm sure you can get it!

9. *To* is a linking word, which points to a double definition. *Travel by air* is the first definition and *annoying insect* is the second.

12. Double definition clues can sometimes clue quite long words — the answer to this one has nine letters! *Bewitches* is the first definition, *with* is the linking word and *ways in* (meaning doors into a venue) is the second definition.

13. *Wrench* is the first definition and *despicable fool* is the second. *Despicable* could conceivably be an anagram indicator, but the letter count (4) helps here — the letters to be rearranged must appear 'in the open' in an anagram clue (refer to Chapter 2 for more detail).

14. *Zero* is a particular score in tennis, and *affection* is the second definition.

Down

1. The answer can be defined as *inflame*, and also as *joss stick*.

2. *Smoke meat* is the first definition and *to* is the linking word. *Restore to health* is the second definition (but you knew that already, didn't you?!).

4. You already know this is a double definition clue, so have a go at putting a 'mental comma' between various words of the clue to see if the two definitions fall out nicely. *Bring, up hind part* doesn't work and neither does *bring up hind, part*. However (chances are you're there before me!), *bring up, hind part* works perfectly! The answer starts with R.

5. *Repeats mindlessly* is the first definition and *bright birds* is the second one. Ignore the punctuation and capital letter!

8. Because a few more words are offered in this clue, try adding the 'mental comma' again. *Don't, sink cash for expenses* doesn't really work, nor does *don't sink cash, for expenses.* The right split in this case is *don't sink* as the first definition, and *cash for expenses* as the second.

10. *Leading lady* is the first definition and *celestial body* (an astronomical term) is the second definition. *With* is a linking word.

11. This clue is a bit trickier because you need to know a bit of ancient Greek mythology to solve it (time to pull out your reference books!). The apostrophe s can be expanded to say that *Greek nymph is* also *reflection*. The answer starts with E.

Crossword answer

Chapter **9**

Revealing Hidden Words

S ome great little cryptic clues are nice and easy to solve. These are hidden word clues, where the answer is actually written out for you, in clear view (well, okay, hidden a bit), within the clue! Like an anagram clue, the actual letters to use in the answer are contained in the clue text — however, unlike an anagram clue, they're not even scrambled up!

In this chapter, I cover all you need to know about searching out hidden word clues and provide a sample crossword that uses this type of clue.

Hunting out Hidden Words

Hidden word clues consist of a definition, an indicator word or two, and some words that hold the answer letters, in order. The word may be split between several words or contained within a longer word.

Here's an example of a hidden word clue:

Big cat was in aioli, once (4)

Big cat is the definition, *in* is the hidden word indicator and the answer is within *aioLI ONce*! As with most cryptic clues, with hidden word clues just ignore things like commas, dashes, hyphens and capital letters.

Here's another example:

In strife at heron's plumage (7)

The word *in* is the hidden word indicator here. Look for a seven-letter series of letters *in* the words *strife at heron's*, for a word that means *plumage*. Did you find it? *striFE AT HERon's*.

Hidden word indicators are words that give a sense of something being hidden in, contained in or held by: *Among, covers, employed by, feature of, held by, hidden in, in, living in, part of, shows, shrouded in, some of, to some extent* and *within* are some options. Container indicators can also be used (these are discussed in Chapter 4).

Sometimes hidden words are hidden within the clue in reverse, so the letter pattern has been written backwards. So, for example, ANGER might be snuck into *raRE GNAt*. Typical indicator words for this situation include: *set back, in retrospect* and *caught up in* (for a down clue). Here's an example of this sort of clue:

Dried fruit is caught up in diet advice (4)

Caught up in tells you to look inside the other words of the clue, and read the letters backwards. You know the answer is four letters long, so scan through the clue to find a four-letter reversed word. *Dried fruit* is the definition. Did you spot it? Yes, it's DATE (*diET ADvice*).

The only pity about these clues is they're deemed to be so easy that most cryptic crosswords only have a couple of them, and some have none. While most setters are happy to put a few 'gimmes' into a puzzle to help you get started, that's about it!

You may occasionally come across some rare variations on hidden word clues. The first of these is the alternate letter clue. In this variety, the answer is hidden in the clue as the alternate letters.

They're generally indicated as either the even letters or the odd letters. For example, FUN can be hidden as the odd letters within fluent — **FlUeNt**. Indicators such as *alternating*, *alternatively*, *even*, *evenly*, *odds*, *oddly* and *regularly* point to this device. These sorts of alternate letter clues generally have short words as answers.

And, finally, hidden letter clues may involve the answer being hidden within the initial letters of the words of the clue. So, for example, CARBON could be encrypted as the initial letters of *cute albatross rests beside orange nest*. Few indicator words are used for this sort of clue; *initially* is the main one.

Uncovering and Solving Hidden Words

TIP

Here's my advice for seeking out hidden words:

» If you notice some indicator words that give a sense of something being within something else, check the letter count and look for a series of letters that provides a synonym for the definition.

» Ignore punctuation and spaces — just look at the letters across words.

» Usually only one or two of these clues are used in a cryptic crossword, so if you've already found a couple, you can probably stop looking for this device in the remaining clues.

» If you see words such as *oddly* or *evenly*, check the alternate letters through the clue, to see if the answer is hidden in this way.

» Look for very long clues because they sometimes fall into this clue category. A very short clue, of only two or three words, is less likely to contain a hidden word.

WARNING

It's easy to get confused between hidden word and container clues, as the indicator words can be identical.

Hidden Words Crossword

Across

1. Shiny mineral is part of totem
I carved (4)

3. Accept orders within adobe yurt (4)

7. Bush oddly found in sphere,
unbroken (5)

8. Mini lute contains nothing (3)

9. Wool fat found in tequila — no
linseed (7)

13. Black liquid held in back by
pirates (3)

14. Superior ones living in brothel,
it emerges (5)

16. Number held by Yukon in
England (4)

17. Regularly kneel, wet, to see an
amphibian (4)

Down

1. Steam is seen initially in many iron
spray treatments (4)

2. Wheels seen in chairs, oddly (3)

4. Sydney beach shrouded in scrub on
ditch (5)

5. Caught up in triple Yule yell (4)

6. To some extent, stab Dom Enfield's
belly (7)

10. Even in damp brook need a
protective garment (5)

11. UK school is part of magneto
network (4)

12. Fool around — jeers etc. regularly (4)

15. Anger idiotic race executives,
initially (3)

Clue explanations

Across

1. *Is part of* is the hidden word indicator in this clue. *Shiny mineral* is the definition.

3. *Within* is the hidden word indicator; *accept orders* is the definition.

7. *Oddly* is the indicator here, and it means to look at the odd numbered letters in another part of the clue (that is, the first, third, fifth letter and so on). *Found in* is the hidden word indicator. *Bush* is the definition.

8. *Nothing* is the definition and *contains* is the hidden word indicator.

9. *Wool fat* is the definition. *Found in* are the hidden word indicator words and looking in *tequila — no linseed* reveals the answer.

13. *Black liquid* is the definition. *Held in back* is the indicator, telling you to look at the letters of the clue, backwards. Ignore that punctuation!

14. *Superior ones* is the definition. *It emerges* is the hidden word indicator.

16. *Number* is the definition. *Held by* is the indicator, which means the answer is hidden within the words *Yukon in England*.

17. *Regularly* is the indicator, telling you to look at every other letter. The clue doesn't specify whether to look at odd or even letters — you have to figure that out for yourself. *Amphibian* is the definition.

Down

1. *Steam* is the definition and *seen initially in* is the hidden word indicator, telling you to look at the initial letters of the wordplay section of the clue.

2. *Wheels* is the definition. *Oddly* is the indicator, so look at the odd numbered letters in the clue until you discover the answer (that is, look at the first, third and fifth letters).

4. *Sydney beach* is the definition. *Shrouded in* is the indicator, which means that the answer can be discovered hiding among the letters of *scrub on ditch*.

5. *Yell* is the definition. *Caught up in* is a reverse hidden word indicator, so look backwards through the letters of *triple yule* to find the four-letter answer.

6. *To some extent* is the hidden word indicator and *belly* is the definition. Ignore the punctuation and capital letters!

10. *Even in* tells you to look at the even numbered letters within *damp brook need*. *A protective garment* is the definition.

11. *UK school* is the definition. *Is part of* is the hidden word indicator. *Magneto network* are the words to hunt around in.

12. *Fool around* is the definition and *regularly* is a hidden word indicator, telling you to look at alternate letters in the rest of the clue, *jeers etc*.

15. *Anger* is the definition and *initially* is the indicator. Look at the initial letters from the rest of the clue, *idiotic race executives*.

Crossword answer

Chapter **10**

Letter Gathering: Abbreviations and Other Oddments

ryptic clue setters often need a way of specifying just a few letters in a clue, to get it to work out or to read well. These 'extra letters' aren't words in their own right. They're mostly used in combination with other clue devices, such as anagrams, charades, deletions or containers, and tend to add to the complexity of clues. If you can identify these 'extra letters', or you see a common 'abbreviation word', you can also determine which part of the clue is the definition.

Proper nouns and short foreign words may be used in cryptic crossword clues. And whole dictionaries are devoted to the weird and wonderful (well, okay, mostly weird) ways that abbreviations are used in cryptic clues.

In this chapter, I show you the more common ways that letters are gathered and added to clues, and provide a sample crossword that uses clues with these kinds of letter-adding devices.

Most of the time, the letters being added are just clued in sequence with the rest of the clue, without any indicator (as is often seen in charade clues — refer to Chapter 3). Occasionally, a short indicator word is offered (such as *and* or *with*), but most of the time no indicator word is used. You just need to remember to look at each word in a cryptic clue separately, checking if any of them can be turned into abbreviations or other letter groups.

Naming Proper Nouns

When reading cryptic clues, you may occasionally come across the names of people or places now and then. So, how best to understand these names in clues? Well, for starters, they may not be names at all! The setter may be disguising a common verb or noun by just adding a capital letter, to make the surface meaning look like a noun and make you think of a person (rather than the word's real meaning). So, if you come across one of the many 'names that are words', like *Bob*, *Grace*, *Mark* and *Violet*, make sure you give some thought to whether these names might *actually* mean *duck down*, *elegance*, *stain* and *purple*!

Various proper nouns crop up in cryptic clues as legitimate names. Capital cities are popular, especially those with short names, such as OSLO, ADEN, SUVA, BONN and RIGA, among many others. Rivers are popular too: The DEE, ELY, ORD, TYE, ARNO, AVON, EXE and PO are just a few.

Members of the Greek and Roman pantheons are sometimes seen: ZEUS, HERA, ARES, EOS, JUNO, SOL and other mythical beings with (generally) short names. Other mythologies are sometimes represented, such as BAAL (the chief Phoenician god) and RA (the Egyptian sun god).

You're likely to also see famous historical figures, actors, sports stars, authors, or literary or biblical characters mentioned from time to time. Shakespearean characters are quite popular. As are Snow White's Seven Dwarves! So a clue that talks about the *Fairy Queen* is probably clueing the letters MAB (Queen Mab, mentioned in Shakespeare's *Romeo and Juliet*, appears from the 17th century onwards). One rule that's followed (more or less), though, is that people who are still alive aren't included in a cryptic clue — the newspapers don't want to risk any chance of libel. (Not all papers follow this, though, and some are more risqué in what they allow.)

If a famous name is used, whether the first or last name, the other half of the person's name forms part of the clue answer. These clues should only be used if it's really clear who the person is. For example, *Capone* in a clue leads to AL and *Sir Edward* = ELGAR. However, *Tony* = BLAIR isn't fair, because there are many other Tonys — including BENNETT, HAWK and CURTIS.

Sometimes you just see *girl*, *girl's name*, *boy* or *boy's name* in a clue, and this clues any short name — such as JOE, IRIS, MAY, ED, TOM, SUE, EVE, BILL . . . the list goes on! Unfortunately, *girl*, *boy* or *name* isn't a precise definition or synonym, and you just have to try a number of names before you find one that fits. While these sorts of clue devices do appear (so I need to tell you about them), I agree with you — they really aren't fair.

Sometimes a longer name in a clue means you need to use the shortened version of the name, so *Edward* = ED, *Diana* = DI, *Patrick* = PAT and so on. These are sometimes indicated with an extra word such as *little*, *short* or similar, so you know that the name has to be shortened.

Just as an example of how varied the ways of clueing a set of letters can be, DON can be clued as *fellow*, *tutor* (both referring to a British university lecturer), *mafia boss*, *Donald* (abbreviated), a *Spanish gentleman*, *Bradman* (the cricketer) or *River* (in the UK)!

REMEMBER

In most cases where proper nouns are used within cryptic clues, the names are simply a way of clueing a set of letters and adding them to the wordplay section of the clue to get to the answer. Occasionally, the name may in fact be the definition, and the answer to the whole clue is a name of some sort. In this case, the wordplay half of the clue also leads to the same name.

Here's an example of a clue that uses a proper noun:

Maiden, wearing Italian flower, beams (6)

In this example, a 'language abuse' word is used. (Refer to Chapter 8 for more on these words.). *Flower* stands for 'something that flows' — that is, a river. A famous *Italian river* is the TIBER. *Maiden* is abbreviated to M (a cricket abbreviation). *Wearing* is a container indicator, so the M is *wearing* the letters of TIBER (making TIMBER). You find a word that also means *beams*.

Here's another example:

Masculine liberal hugged by Ms West (4)

Hugged is a container indicator. *Liberal* indicates the letter L. *Ms West* = MAE. Put MAE around (that is, hugging) the L and you get a word (MALE) that also means *masculine*.

See the section 'Affixing Abbreviations' for more on common abbreviations.

Speaking in Tongues

Another way that setters like to add letters to a clue is by using foreign words (see the preceding section for how proper nouns are used to do the same). The foreign words used are always well-known words and generally very short. These words are indicated with a label, so you know what country they're from (*in Spain*, *from Paris* or *German*, for example), or may just generally say something like *across the (English) Channel*, *foreign*, *abroad*, *in Europe*, *European* or *on the Continent*. French is particularly popular.

Words such as *and*, *the*, simple greetings, numbers and very basic vocabulary are the usual words to be translated, and a simple phrase book or online translator solves any of these translations, if you don't remember them from high school.

Some examples of how these words could be clued include the following:

dear in Lyon = CHER (French for *dear*)

French sea = MER (French for *sea*)

one in Köln = EIN (German for *one*)

and German = UND (German for *and*)

the Spanish = EL (Spanish for *the*)

Here's a full clue that uses a foreign word:

The French fool's lake (6)

Lake is the definition. This is a charade clue (one part put after the other). *The French* is another way of defining the French word for *the*. There are a few options — LA is the one used here. Add on a synonym for *fool* (GOON) to get the answer: LAGOON. The apostrophe s on *fool* doesn't indicate possession (the *lake* belonging to the *fool*), but is an abbreviation of *is*. It's saying the wordplay (*the French fool*) *is* another way of saying *lake*.

Affixing Abbreviations

Cryptic abbreviations are widely used in cryptic clues and often trip up new solvers. Learning to spot them in clues takes a bit of practice — but acquiring this skill is vital to your success as a solver.

Setters have thousands of ways to indicate a letter or two (or three) in a cryptic clue, so you're likely to sometimes need a crossword dictionary or online list for some help (some resources are listed in Chapter 18). In fact, even the basic list of abbreviations I've put together for you is quite long, so I've put it into the Appendix.

Another way setters can indicate single letters is by noting them as the capital letter of something. So *the capital for Italy*, for example, might be clueing the letter I (the first letter of Italy), rather than ROME!

TIP

Many abbreviations are 'obvious' everyday ones, such as K for *kilo*, L for *left*, R for *right*, C for *Celsius*, N for *north* and ED for *editor*, and you can find these in any dictionary. Just look at the initial letter entry for each letter in the dictionary, and the entry lists common abbreviations for that letter.

Other commonly used abbreviations are things like the periodic table (*carbon* = C, *gold* = AU), the phonetic alphabet (*tango* = T), Roman numerals (51 = LI), international country codes or licence plate codes (*Somalia* = SO, *Germany* = D, for Deutschland), state abbreviations (*Tasmania* = TAS, *Colorado* = CO), date abbreviations (*Wednesday* = W or WED, *December* = DEC) and scientific units (*farad* = F).

There is a massive list of more bizarre abbreviations. Some of these may make sense, while others are a bit of a stretch of the imagination! Many are UK-centric, so these can take a while to learn if you're not from Britain. Some are rather antiquated too, but do still pop up in clues now and then.

Here are a few examples of these sorts of abbreviations:

>> *Artists* = RA (Royal Academy)
>> *Ball, circle, egg, nothing, ring, zero* = O
>> *Beginner, learner, novice, student* = L (learner)
>> *Big, very large, outsize* = OS (for outsize, a UK clothing size)
>> *Castle* = R (for rook) and *queen* = Q and other chess notations
>> *Duck* = O, *run* = R, *maiden* = M and other cricketing terms
>> *Direction, point, quarter* = N, S, E or W (compass points)
>> *Embarrassed* = RED
>> *First class, high class, top class* = AI (in other words, A1, with the 1 read as letter I)
>> *Forte/loud* = F, *piano/soft* = P, *soprano* = S, *clef* = C or F, and other musical terms
>> *Graduate, scholar, degree* = BA (Bachelor of Arts) or MA (Master of Arts)
>> *Hesitation* = ER or UM
>> *King* or *Queen* = ER (*Edwardus Rex* or *Elizabetha Regina*)
>> *Kiss* = X
>> *Love* = O (from the tennis score of 0)
>> *Model* = T (from Model T Ford!)
>> *Old boy* = OB

>> *Sailor* = AB (able-bodied seaman), SALT, TAR

>> *String* = E, A, D, G (violin strings)

>> *This era* = AD

>> *Upper class, posh, high class, uppish* = U

REMEMBER

Having a good grasp of abbreviations is essential to cracking the cryptic clue code, so I encourage you to check out the list in the Appendix, and read each word in a cryptic clue closely, seeing if any of them lead to an abbreviation.

Crossing Clues

Very occasionally you may see a number used in a clue that doesn't lead to a Roman numeral . . . what are these? They may well be a cross-reference to another clue in the crossword! These are generally rare clues, and can only be written if a neat crossover occurs between one word in the grid and another.

If the number is unique in the clue list (that is, it's only an across or a down word, not both), the setter may only indicate it with the clue number. Otherwise, A or across, or D or down, may be included to indicate across or down, respectively. A cross-referenced clue means that you need to find the answer to the referenced clue first, and then use that word to solve the second clue.

Here's a quick example of this, using two random clue numbers:

8 across: *Endless loathing for head covering* (3)

2 down: *Gossip around 8* (4)

The first clue says that a *head covering* can be found from *loathing* (HATE) without its last letter (*endless*) = HAT

The second clue is a charade clue, that says another word for *gossip* can be found with *around* (C, for circa) and the answer to clue 8 (HAT) = CHAT.

UNDERSTANDING XIMENEAN AND LIBERTARIAN CLUES

Two camps exist within cryptic cross-word setters: Those who follow 'Ximenean principles' and those who write 'non-Ximenean' or 'Libertarian' clues.

So, who is this Ximenes, you ask? Good question! Ximenes was the pseudonym of Derrick Somerset Macnutt (1902–1971), one of the early cryptic crossword setters from England. (Many cryptic setters use pseudonyms — Macnutt's namesake, Ximenes, was a Grand Inquisitor in the Spanish Inquisition. Others just sign their work with their initials. Some newspapers remove all identifiers from all their crosswords, so their puzzles appear anonymously.)

Ximenes started writing cryptic crosswords in 1939, quite soon after the first cryptic was printed in the UK. You may think that modern cryptics are difficult to solve, but many of the earliest cryptics were impossibly hard, and often unfair to the solver. Ximenes' major contribution to the field was to establish the rules of fair play, cluemanship, grid construction and the different types of clues used. He wrote the seminal book, *Ximenes on the Art of the Crossword*, in 1966, which is still an important book in this arena today.

Fellow setter Jonathan Crowther (Azed) said that a good cryptic clue should contain three elements:

- A precise definition
- A fair subsidiary indication (what I've been calling the *wordplay*)
- Nothing else

A clue that follows the principles set out by Ximenes is said to be *Ximenean*. The clues in this book follow Ximenean principles, and the descriptions of the different clue devices are Ximenean too.

Non-Ximenean or *Libertarian* styles of writing cryptic have also developed over the years (shock horror!). These clues don't follow some of the guidelines set out by Ximenes, are often a bit more relaxed in how they're written and are more likely to be seen in the less 'formal' cryptic crosswords. *Araucaria* (John Galbraith Graham — *Araucaria* is the genus of the Monkey-puzzle Tree!) is a noted Libertarian setter, and his clues are known for being witty and clever.

A Libertarian clue may only 'roughly' get the message across to you, and may not have such rigorous or 'formal' use of cryptic indicators. A lot of Libertarian devices are used in the way abbreviations are written or how letters are indicated within a word, and you may sometimes come across them. Here are some of the other things a Libertarian cryptic crossword may hold:

- The word to be turned into an anagram is not written in the clear (refer to Chapter 2), but is a *synonym* for the word to be scrambled up. This is called an *indirect anagram*. Most setters do try to avoid indirect anagrams, though.

- The wordplay may say to put the letters of A into B, but you actually have to put the letters of B into A.

- A proper name may be clued without a capital letter (so using the Mae West example used in this chapter, her surname could be written as *west* instead of *West*).

- They may have more linking or superfluous words in the clue.

- Wordplay is often hidden in unexpected ways within a clue and you have to add spaces to words to get at it. In general, these ought to be indicated with a question mark in the clue, so you know you need to read the words a bit differently. For example, *indeed* in the wordplay may mean put something *in* DEED. Or *infer* means put something *in* FER, *not* = *no* T (delete the T from another word in the wordplay) or *exploits* = PISTOL (*ex* indicates an anagram, working on *ploits* — which in my view is entirely unfair).

- They may indicate letters in unorthodox ways. For example, *midnight* = G (the *mid*dle letter of *night*), *firstborn* = B (the *first* letter of *born*) or *finally* = Y (the *final* letter of *ly*).

These clues and devices are often hotly debated on cryptic crossword forums, and passionate cryptic buffs often fall into one camp or the other as to which they prefer and how much language abuse they tolerate. While Ximenean clues are generally more fair and solvable than Libertarian ones, I think it's important for the field to continue to develop and modernise. Seeing new wordplay devices and tricks is exciting (so long as they're fair to solvers). Very neat clues can be written in either camp, as well as bad clues, after all!

Many regular cryptics have a mix of Ximenean and Libertarian clues, and setters and newspapers vary in how 'Libertarian' they are, so keep an eye out for these devices.

Letter Gathering Crossword

Across

1. Purple-brown chalice flipped over string (4)

3. Soprano has pale waterbird (4)

7. Railway a supporter of women (3)

8. Best prize comes from Conifer Street (5)

9. Cooking instructions: Pierce wildly and add sulphur (7)

13. Bachelor inside, tucked in to cool off (5)

15. Environmentally friendly eastern firm (3)

16. Capone announced a hot drink with round singing voice (4)

17. Saint Silver is a deer (4)

Down

1. Quiet bus smashed up taverns (4)

2. Walking stick includes right lifting gear (5)

4. Conflict from Perth's state castle (3)

5. Observe heavy weight going north east (4)

6. Policeman not working with the Sorbet Queen (7)

10. First woman to book a function (5)

11. The French have five good molten rocks (4)

12. Picard's foe's king caught in quagmire (4)

14. Answer loud model at back of the ship (3)

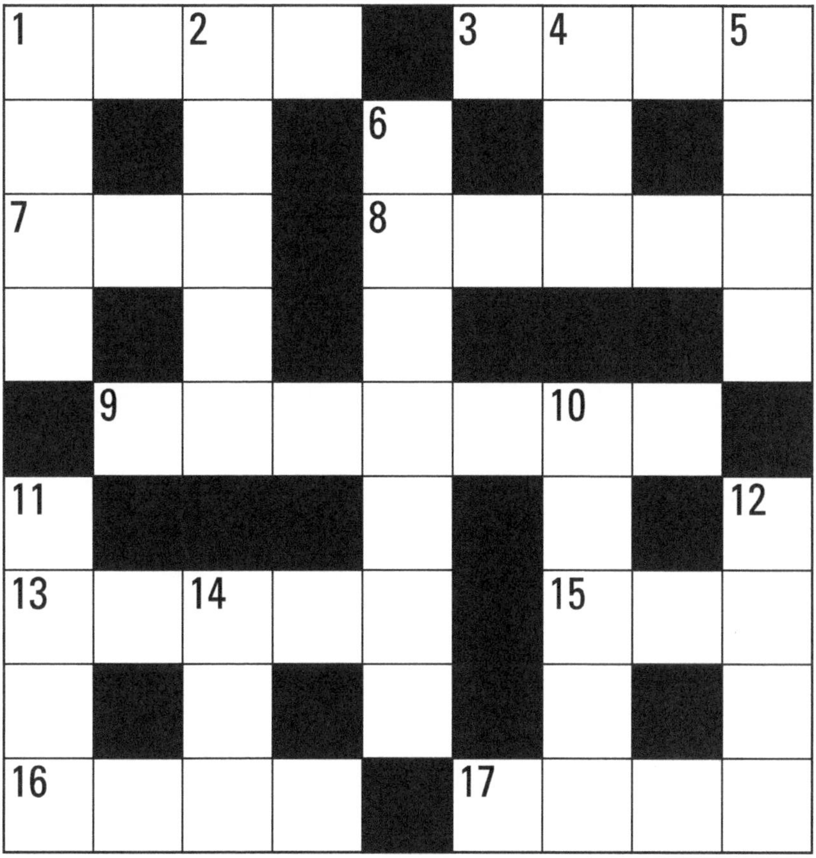
1
2
3
4
5
6
7
8
9
10
11
12
13
14
15
16
17

Clue explanations

Across

1. *Purple-brown* is the definition. A *chalice* is a CUP and *flipped over* is a reversal indicator. This gives you PUC (CUP backwards). Then add E (a violin *string*).

3. This is a charade clue (one bit added to another, in order). *Soprano* is abbreviated as S. The S *has* WAN (pale). *Waterbird* is the definition.

7. *Railway* is abbreviated as BR (for British Rail), and just add on A (*a*, in plain view) to get a word that also means *supporter of women*. This is another charade clue.

8. *Best prize* is the definition. Therefore, the rest of the clue is the wordplay! *Comes from* are linking words. *Conifer* is a FIR and *Street* is abbreviated as ST. Ignore the capital letters.

9. *Wildly* is an anagram indicator and the letters of *pierce* are what to scramble up. Then add on an abbreviation for *sulphur* (S) to find another word *for* the definition, *cooking instructions*.

13. *Bachelor* (BA) is put *inside* (container indicator) ATE (*tucked in*). *Cool off* is the definition.

15. *Environmentally friendly* is the definition. This clue is a charade clue, so just put the parts together in order. *Eastern* is abbreviated as E and *firm* is abbreviated as CO (company).

16. *Capone* clues the letters AL (the gangster). Add on a little homophone — *announced a hot drink* tells you to say a word for a *hot drink* (tea) aloud. This gets you the letter T. Add on (*with*) an O (*round*) to get to a word meaning a *singing voice*.

17. *Saint* is abbreviated as ST. *Silver* is abbreviated as AG (and why on earth is abbreviated such a long word?!). *Is a* are linking words and *deer* is the definition.

Down

1. *Quiet* = P (piano = soft/quiet in music). Add on an anagram of BUS *smashed up* (anagram indicator). This equals another word for *taverns*.

2. This is a container clue. *Walking stick* (CANE) *includes* (container indicator) *right* (R). *Lifting gear* is the definition.

4. *Conflict* is the definition and it also means *Perth's state* (WA, for Western Australia) + R for *castle* (which is also a rook — abbreviated as R in chess terminology). *From* is the linking word in this charade clue (one word after another).

5. *Observe* is the definition. A *heavy weight* is a TON. *Going north* is a down clue reversal indicator, so write TON from south to north (that is, backwards) and add *east* — E, in this instance. Note that you need to resist the natural impulse to put *north east* together as a compass direction!

6. *Policeman* is the definition in this charade clue. *Not working* is OFF, put it *with* ICE (*sorbet*) and R (*queen* = R comes from Regina, the Latin word for queen).

10. *First woman* = EVE. It goes *to* NT for *book* (New Testament) to get a solution that also means *function*.

11. *The French* is LA (*the* in *French*). *Have* is a linking word in this charade clue. *Five* = V (Roman numeral) + A (*good*, think of A Grade), for another way of writing *molten rocks*.

12. *Picard's foe's* is the definition, using possessive s in two ways! *Picard's foe is* is how to read this (possessive s, followed by contraction of *foe is*). *King* is abbreviated as R (for Rex, the Latin word for king), which is *caught in* (container indicator) BOG (*quagmire*).

14. *Answer* is abbreviated as A. *Loud* = F (forte in music) and *model* = T (Huh?! Model T Ford is very common in cryptics, so whenever you see *model*, think of T!). *At back of the ship* is the definition.

> How did you go? This teaching crossword has normal cryptic clues, with a range of different devices — albeit with a lot of names and abbreviations. If you got through this crossword without having to refer to the other chapters or answers, well done!

P	U	C	E	■	S	W	A	N
U	■	R	■	O	■	A	■	O
B	R	A	■	F	I	R	S	T
S	■	N	■	F	■	■	■	E
■	R	E	C	I	P	E	S	■
L	■	■	■	C	■	V	■	B
A	B	A	T	E	■	E	C	O
V	■	F	■	R	■	N	■	R
A	L	T	O	■	S	T	A	G

Chapter **11**
Enjoying Cryptics Around the Globe

The cryptic crossword originated in England and eventually spread to other countries. (Refer to Chapter 1 for more on this.) Cryptics are also popular in Australia, New Zealand, Ireland, India, Canada, the Netherlands, Kenya and South Africa (as well as plenty of other countries, of course!). The past crossword editor of the *Daily Telegraph*, Val Gilbert, said that she only ever came across one country that hadn't heard of cryptic crosswords, and that was the Soviet Union!

While gathering precise information on the 'state of play' with cryptics in all of these places is difficult, in this chapter I can share a few interesting things with you about regional differences.

Looking at Cryptics in the United Kingdom

The United Kingdom is the birthplace of the cryptic crossword, so has the longest history of cryptic writing and is the source of all the major treatises on how to construct cryptics and the rules of 'fair play' (refer to Chapter 10).

Different levels of difficulty exist in cryptics published in United Kingdom newspapers. Generally, the more 'popular' the publication, the easier the cryptic. The *Times* cryptic crosswords are hard and are strictly Ximenean (refer to Chapter 10). The *Times* cryptic is written by a group of around a dozen experienced setters (who also publish their work elsewhere). The *Times* cryptics are traditionally published anonymously.

Some of the perceived elitism of the 'cryptic club' seems to have arisen from the use of some very difficult clues that rely on a very good classical education, requiring an in-depth knowledge of literature, classical mythology and poetry. These sorts of clues were more common in older cryptic crosswords and aren't as widespread any more.

British cryptics draw on the names of local villages, towns, rivers, mountains, London landmarks and suburbs, Underground stations and even local politicians' names. UK abbreviations are also very regional, and can be rather dated (lots from the 1940s and 1950s). If you're not from the United Kingdom, these clues can be very challenging to crack because you don't have the assumed local knowledge.

Some clue devices are only seen occasionally in cryptics, and I haven't covered some of these rarer clues in this book in any detail. They generally make cryptics even harder, and many of these clues are more often seen in British cryptics than in those written elsewhere. These include

- ❯❯ Cryptic Definition clues (covered in this section)
- ❯❯ &lit clues (covered in this section)
- ❯❯ Pun clues, which are one step up from homophone clues, and involve more than one word and unusual pronunciation
- ❯❯ Quotation clues (that require you to fill in the missing word of the quotation or poem)
- ❯❯ Literary Allusion clues, for which a wide literary knowledge is needed
- ❯❯ Cockney clues (typically using the Cockney accent — where, for example, the starting H of a word is dropped — or using Cockney rhyming slang; these are also mentioned in Chapter 7)

- ➤ Spoonerism clues, where initial letters are transposed (as in *runny babbits* instead of *bunny rabbits*)
- ➤ The use of Scottish, Welsh and Irish words in clues
- ➤ The use of British-centric abbreviations (such as U for *upper class*)

Because they're rather clever, the following sections give you a little information on *cryptic definition* and *&lit* clues. If you really get into cryptics, many resources can help you to decode these tricky clues (see Chapter 18). I also cover advanced cryptics, which use a particular device within the grid overall, and non-symmetrical barred grids.

Cryptic definition clues

Wait, isn't this *whole book* about cryptic clues? Yes, but . . . these ones are special. The whole clue is a straightforward definition of the answer, but only if you read it the right way! Hence the *cryptic definition* title. They're often indicated with a question mark.

No wordplay, as such, is involved — no way of putting letters and words together to form the letters of the answer. You just have to read the clue in a lateral way and see if the answer falls out! No specific indicator can be found and no secondary way to figure out the clue out exists — perhaps not surprisingly, the answers to these clues are often the last ones to be solved in a grid.

Here are a few examples (from other tricky setters):

Return payment? (6) = RANSOM

Sleep soundly? (5) = SNORE (sleep while making sound)

His downfall was shattering (6,6) = HUMPTY DUMPTY

&lit clues

And literally so is the full name of *&lit*. &lit clues, sometimes called *double duty* clues, are another rarity, but special when they do work out.

The whole clue is both the definition and the wordplay. So, you read the clue one way to get the wordplay from it (the usual devices like anagrams and charades), and then a second time literally (paying attention to the surface meaning, for once!) to get the definition. These clues are often marked with an exclamation mark at the end.

Here's an example (by a setter cleverer than me!):

Cop in male form! (9) = POLICEMAN

The whole clue is the definition of a POLICEMAN, isn't it? But wait, there's more! (Sorry, no steak knives.) *Form* is an anagram indicator and when you scramble up the letters of *cop in male*, guess what? Yup. POLICEMAN. Nice, isn't it?!

And another example:

A place where you can display a vice among company! (6) = CASINO

Read the surface meaning of this clue and it does indeed act as a good (if rather oblique) definition of CASINO. Now for the wordplay — *a vice* is also A SIN. Put these letters *among* (container indicator) CO (*company*) to get C-ASIN-O. Same result!

Advanced cryptics and barred grids

The Brits also developed advanced or thematic cryptics, where another device is at play in the grid overall — for example, all the eight-letter answers might have their clues presented in random order (not against the correct clue number).

These sorts of difficult cryptics are usually set in a non-symmetrical barred grid, where the start and ends of words are indicated with thick black lines, instead of black squares. Figure 11-1 shows an example of a barred grid. As you can see, a great deal of overlapping of the words in the grid occurs — almost every letter is checked. This makes the grid easier to solve (and harder to compile!). As a result, setters feel safe in providing much harder clues, because they know the solver gets a lot of help from the crossing-over words. These sorts of grids also tend to use much more obscure words and complicated wordplay.

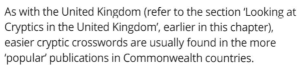

Checking Cryptics in the Commonwealth

Cryptic crosswords spread from the United Kingdom to other Commonwealth countries, where they still flourish today. Here's a look at where you can access some cryptic crosswords:

>> Australian Lovatts Publications produces a vast array of puzzle magazines, including cryptic crossword magazines. Lovatts puzzles are published widely in Australia, New Zealand, Ireland and the United Kingdom. Lovatts cryptics are generally very easy to solve, making them a good starting point for those just getting to know cryptics.

>> Women's magazines and 'competition' puzzle books have easy cryptics as well. These puzzles rely more heavily on the easier cryptic devices, such as hidden words (Chapter 9) and anagrams (Chapter 2).

TIP

As with the United Kingdom (refer to the section 'Looking at Cryptics in the United Kingdom', earlier in this chapter), easier cryptic crosswords are usually found in the more 'popular' publications in Commonwealth countries.

>> Newspaper cryptics are next up in difficulty, with the weekly cryptics published in major newspapers being the hardest. These generally appear on the weekends, when you've

presumably got a bit more time to be tormented. Here are some points to note about newspapers that publish cryptic crosswords around the world:

- In general, Australian cryptics tend to be easier than their British counterparts, probably because a 'cryptic crossword culture' isn't as strong, and newspaper editors wish to make the clues more accessible to all readers. The definitions are often easier to spot in Australian cryptic clues. However, difficult Australian cryptics can certainly include *cryptic definition* and *&lit* clues, too (refer to the sections 'Cryptic definition clues' and '&lit clues', earlier in this chapter). Many Australian papers publish British cryptics, though.

- Several papers in Canada carry cryptics. *The Globe and Mail* publishes a daily cryptic that's moderately easy. This puzzle is also published with a set of 'quick clues' (that lead to the same answers), which is a great help to those just learning about cryptics.

- In India, *The Hindu* newspaper publishes daily cryptic crosswords.

- New Zealand and South Africa also have papers that regularly carry cryptics.

- Most, if not all, non-British newspapers that include cryptic crosswords use local cryptic setters, as well as importing puzzles from overseas setters (especially from the United Kingdom).

Getting to Know Cryptics in the United States

Cryptics were introduced to the United States by Broadway composer Stephen Sondheim. He's a big fan of games in general, and in 1968 and 1969 he regularly contributed a witty cryptic crossword to the *New York* magazine. Some years after this debut, a few other publications picked up cryptics as well — *Harper's* in 1976 and *The Atlantic Monthly* in 1977.

Only a few setters regularly create cryptics in the United States, and only a few papers and magazines regularly publish cryptics (including *The New York Times*, *Games* magazine and *Dell Magazine*).

American crossword editors have a slightly different set of rules by which setters have to abide. Anagram and hidden word clues are used more frequently than in cryptics from the United Kingdom, which can make them easier to solve. *Cryptic definition* clues are generally not allowed (but are used in 'normal' American crosswords), and a few other more technical limitations exist that make writing cryptic clues harder for the setter, but easier for the solver — which is good news for you!

WHAT MAKES A CLUE HARD?

Understanding that cryptic crosswords can be relatively easy or really hard is pretty easy. But what is it that makes them so? After all, every cryptic clue has the same basic anatomy of definition + wordplay both giving the same answer.

Several aspects are at play here. For starters, hard cryptics usually have harder words in the grid, so the answers to the clues may be more archaic or obscure words, and require a much wider vocabulary and more scholarly knowledge. Definitions of the words in a hard clue may be a more 'oblique' definition of the answer (refer to Chapter 1 for a discussion about definitions). Hard UK cryptics can use more local language, names of politicians and obscure local place names, and tougher UK-centric abbreviations, which can present hardships for solvers outside of Britain.

Easier cryptic clues tend to have more words 'in the clear', so you're not required to come up with a synonym for a word, but you can just use the words in the clue as they are. Harder clues more often require you to come up with synonyms. Synonyms may also be less obvious, more oblique or be unusual usages of the word.

Here's an example of this. First, here's the easy version of a clue for MAROON:

Reddish-brown argon found in the moon (6) = put AR (the chemical symbol for *argon*) into MOON = MAROON (a *reddish-brown* colour).

(continued)

(continued)

And here's a harder clue for the same word:

Satellite carries Arabic colour (6) = *satellite* 'carrying' AR (*Arabic*). AR put into *satellite* makes no sense, clearly, but if you put AR into MOON (a synonym for *satellite*), you get to the answer of MAROON.

So, as you can see, requiring this extra step of going from *moon* to *satellite*, and using a less obvious abbreviation for AR, and having a broader definition (*colour*, instead of *reddish-brown*) makes this clue less obvious and, therefore, harder to solve.

A difference can also be seen in the types of clue devices used in harder cryptic crosswords. They are more likely to use things like *augmented anagrams*, where some specified letters from the anagram fodder have to be removed first, before you can start 'anagramming', or substitutions, where one letter is substituted for another. They also may have more parts to the clue than seen in easier crosswords. For example, you may have to string together as many as four or five parts in a charade clue to get to the answer.

Using HORSE as an example, one case of an augmented anagram of HORSE is an anagram of SHOWER with the W removed. An example of a substitution device is clueing HORSE as GORSE with H substituted for the G — substitutions like this are indicated with words such as A *for* B, A *instead of* B, A *replacing* B and so on; basically, any word or phrase that gives the sense of changing one thing for another.

Solving a harder cryptic crossword is still entirely possible, as long as you keep an eye out for the vocabulary differences and the other points above. Don't let them intimidate you!

2

Sample Cryptic Crosswords

In this part, there are some actual cryptic crosswords to try out! There are three difficulty levels for these puzzles: Chapter 12 has eight easy crosswords, Chapter 13 has four medium crosswords, and Chapter 14 has four hard crosswords.

The easy puzzles have — hopefully — easy clues, and I've also given you more help along the way. The definition parts of the clues are highlighted in **bold**, and words that lead to abbreviations are in *italics*.

The Medium crossword clues also have some hints — indicator words are highlighted in **bold**, and as for the easy crosswords, words that lead to abbreviations are in *italics*.

As you've probably guessed by now, I provide no such helping hands with the hard crosswords. Don't fret though, you're not completely on your own — I do provide hints for all of the crosswords in Part 3.

If you would like to solve more of my cryptic crosswords, you might like to check out the companion volume to this book, *Cryptic Crosswords For Dummies*, which has a much bigger collection of crosswords.

Chapter **12**
Easy Peasy Cryptics

This chapter has eight easy crosswords for you to try out with your new-found skills! Please don't feel too nervous about giving them a try; if anything, doing a crossword is easier than solving clues on their own, as you have the additional help from the crossing over words and checked letters to help you.

The crosswords included in this chapter are on a 13 × 13 grid (that is, 13 squares across and 13 squares down). I've included a higher proportion of the easiest clue types (especially those using anagrams and hidden word clues) — definitely more than you would normally find in a newspaper cryptic. These are generally easier to solve, as the letters of the answers are there in plain view (even if they're a bit disguised). A lot of words in the wordplay are 'in clear view' too, so you don't have to look for synonyms.

I've used an everyday vocabulary both in the grids and in the clues. No archaic words, rare place names or oblique definitions here! If you do see the occasional 'hard word', you can be sure that it is either part of an anagram or a hidden word clue. None of the clues require you to have to look for difficult definitions in a dictionary.

These clues have the definition part of the clue highlighted in **bold**, so you can see at a glance which part of each clue is the definition and which part is the wordplay. Words that lead to abbreviations are set in *italics*.

Puzzle 1

Across

1. Scam pariah holds **aperitif** (7)

5. Loose picot **point** (5)

8. **British interviewer** hiding in park in Sonora (9)

9. Propel boat noisily to get **fish eggs** (3)

10. **Set aside** timer that's wound back (5)

12. Is *Oscar* late and **set apart**? (7)

13. Enter main tent, out for **amusement** (13)

15. Inch cog squashes **tiny dumplings** (7)

17. Master missing first **flower** (5)

19. Napoleon shows us **a constellation** (3)

20. Entering a rotten **citrus fruit** (9)

22. Mash pears and **asparagus** (5)

23. Settler beaten up to get **messages** (7)

Down

1. **Dance about** Cape *River* (5)

2. Ram knocked over **ruin** (3)

3. **Pilot** discovered in Yugoslavia, tormented (7)

4. **Uplifting** battered pails into rain (13)

5. Brown, proceed to **dance** (5)

6. Improperly entrap men **long term** (9)

7. **Merciful** *learner* set in cement (7)

11. Frantic memo; tenor supplies **time keeper** (9)

13. Novel fun gels cause **floods** (7)

14. **Tidiest** swallow sat in the roost (7)

16. **Provide food** in public, at Erebus (5)

18. **Staggers** and leers rudely (5)

21. Topless rodents **decorate a cake** (3)

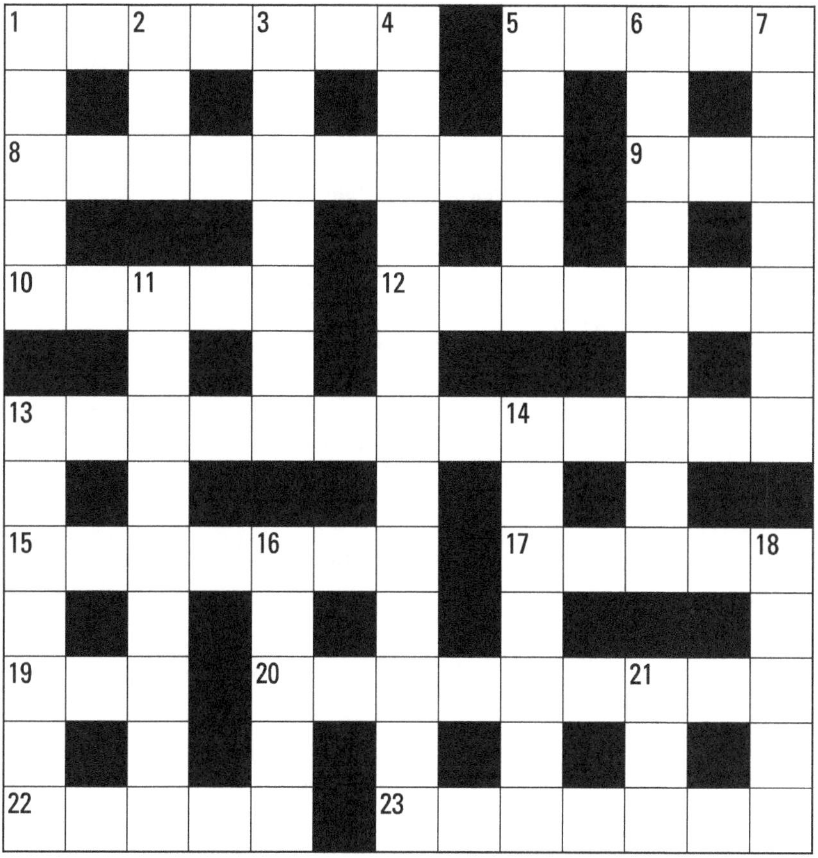
1
2
3
4
5
6
7
8
9
10
11
12
13
14
15
16
17
18
19
20
21
22
23

Puzzle 2

Across

1. Cried, tipped over **drink** (5)

4. Sounds like vegetable **discharge** (4)

7. Soothes loudly, lisp oddly (5)

8. Martin and I make a **cocktail** (7)

10. Sense of self found in this category (3)

11. Orange battered bream (5)

12. Vice can disrupt **immunisation** (7)

14. Spielberg found at wild events (6)

16. Praise part of chic red item (6)

20. Country's *gold* stair broke (7)

23. Loots the cloth bags (5)

25. Short underwater vessel reverses into **public transport** (3)

26. *Delaware* fact has *nothing*, **actually** (2,5)

27. Heads off, noticing **cake decoration** (5)

28. Poses questions, losing track of first disguises (4)

29. Wash out resin accidentally (5)

Down

1. Incorrect lace rib **shell measurement** (7)

2. Severed inaccurate **warrant** (7)

3. Harem overachiever carries **take away** (6)

4. Poetic characters in wobbly rickshaw (5)

5. I bail by mistake and make an **excuse** (5)

6. Biting pest can be heard to run away (4)

9. Still seen in finer tweeds (5)

13. Signal the line, we're told (3)

14. Initially sugar caramelises, and lastly dessert is **put in hot water** (5)

15. Ex-soldier's animal doctor (3)

17. Madly run, as is, with **one from Moscow** (7)

18. Fool's broken *energy* device (7)

19. Research room has our **work** (6)

21. SOS includes a *note* to get **couches** (5)

22. Swings mythical bird a *kilometre south* (5)

24. Wise herb (4)

Puzzle 3

Across

1. **Scented smoke** swirling in scene (7)
5. **Have fun** with a back-to-front lever (5)
8. In April, I lack a **flowering shrub** (5)
9. **Baltic country** exploded into sea (7)
10. *Soprano* in a gap? It's a **wheeze** (4)
11. Distressed lass at US **attacks** (8)
14. **Rent** permit (3)
16. **Deer** announced dessert (5)
17. I hear eight **had dinner** (3)
19. Untidy dim Grace **scowled** (8)
20. **Mail** a strut (4)
23. **Exhibition buildings** deploy among mothers (7)
25. Messy chore to get **earthy pigment** (5)
26. **Herb**'s time on radio (5)
27. *South Poland* has urge to **spend freely** (7)

Down

1. Sounds like an ill bird of prey is **criminal** (7)
2. Confused locust missed *love* in **religious sects** (5)
3. **French resort** is pleasant (4)
4. **Sight organ** reads both ways (3)
5. Converted deer cart **went back along route** (8)
6. **Flavouring** *article* set in villa (7)
7. **Shows the way** to leashes (5)
12. **Beach** is stable, according to hearsay (5)
13. Disturbed irate mum is **childish** (8)
15. *Son* wearing XXX is **longing for a drink** (7)
18. **Drastic** Mex Tree mangled (7)
19. Brolga mutters, hiding **compass** (5)
21. **Alternative** mother is topless (5)
22. **Hurl** a dish (4)
24. **Sibling**'s half of thesis (3)

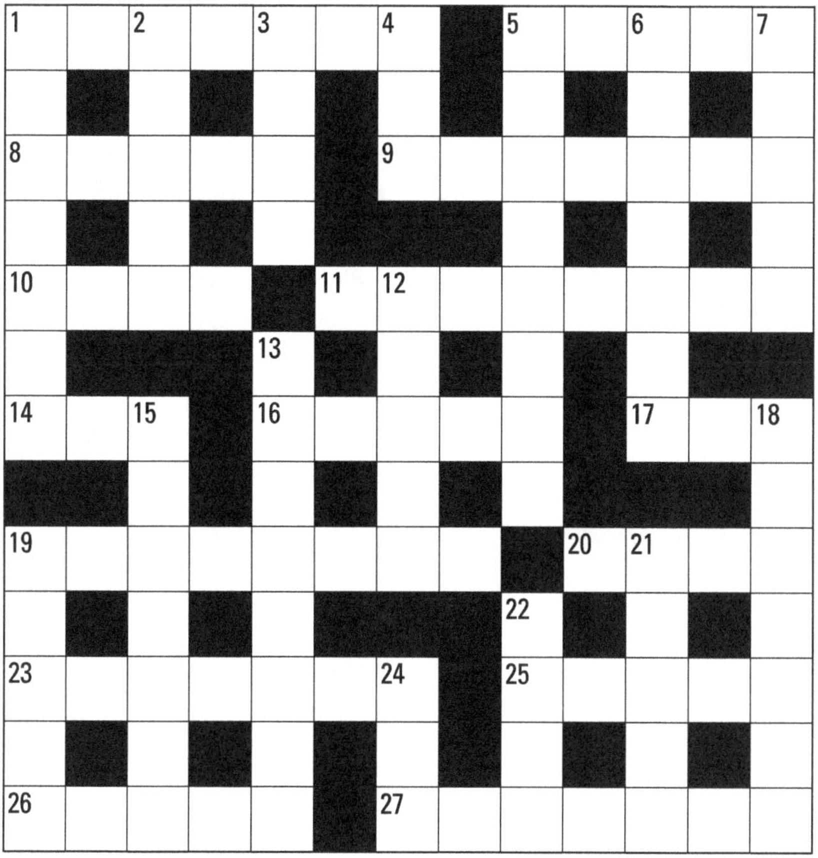

Puzzle 4

Across

1. Grand total of half a possum (3)

3. Sounds like a tax for **pins** (5)

6. Flying mammal hit a ball (3)

8. Shelter unruly CIA Command, too (13)

9. Hauls over coals, but it's chilly in the *ship* (6)

13. *Quiet* noblemen create **round gems** (6)

16. Quick cooked tuna sensation (13)

17. Hornet spoiled **royal seat** (6)

20. Respect some of celeste emulator (6)

24. Edited racial fiction provides an **explanation** (13)

26. Vapour sink runs backwards (3)

27. Get stuck into odd eBay trumps (3,2)

28. Noticed half of the jigsaw (3)

Down

1. Ocean is a feature of Seattle (3)

2. Boiled mocha is **very manly** (5)

3. Subdued Scottish hat *editor* (5)

4. Bird *about* to row (4)

5. Rollerblade ray (5)

6. Wild Rose Bar receives *right iodine* (5)

7. Inclined to cut short **two fives** (3)

10. *Celsius* measurement is **a piece of cake** (5)

11. Pilot to hold **raffle** (5)

12. Burn singer, almost (5)

13. *Learner* fills savoury paste **dish** (5)

14. Very skilled medley taped (5)

15. Parasite lost first blouse (5)

18. *Right* paddles for **bellows** (5)

19. Casino is enough to contain **commotion** (5)

21. Endless small lobsters for **mischievous child** (5)

22. Headless demons expose **sins** (5)

23. Drizzle dropped audibly (4)

24. Toothed wheel in stucco gate (3)

25. Latest newt has its tail cut off (3)

Puzzle 5

Across

1. Lettuce function (3)

3. Haul in cold ragweed (4)

5. Screen the *sulphur* can (4)

9. Blending slime creates **citrus fruits** (5)

10. Fruit garden, or leafy vegetable? (7)

11. Deranged uncles in a trance to attain **semi-transparency** (12)

14. *Duck* exists for **source of oil** (6)

15. A vaguely secure **save** (6)

18. Famous egg's pump duty myth is phoney (6,6)

21. Goes along to chaotic tats den (7)

22. More worn folder lost header (5)

23. Lid flipped over *trainee*, **Herb** (4)

24. Jazzy keen **joint** (4)

25. Regulation is feature of political award (3)

Down

1. Young horse's bad clot (4)

2. Japanese warrior's drunken arias contain a *Greek letter* (7)

3. Tipsy intact fiends supply **antiseptic** (12)

4. Greek god has a survey *round* (6)

6. Somehow, China **linked rings** (5)

7. Bob features in clown odyssey (3)

8. Mutant mice care, once, for a **summer treat** (3,5,4)

12. Pitcher missing leader of fewer (4)

13. Scottish lake's cloche is losing edges (4)

16. Unusual dialect in **fortress** (7)

17. Inventor Thomas knocked out, side on (6)

19. Lead, perhaps, a *tango* in middle of meal (5)

20. Returned hospital room **sketch** (4)

21. Help maid who's lost her head (3)

Puzzle 6

Across

1. Ear parts *exist* among *the Spanish* (5)

4. Taxi and backpack *east* to find **vegetable** (7)

8. Egyptian river lost end for **nought** (3)

9. Armoured animal's funny dill aroma (9)

10. Appointment to meet — attempt on *street* (5)

11. Ordinary *avenue* anger (7)

13. Ponies crackle insanely at **hunting dog** (6, 7)

16. Conductor breaks oar stem (7)

18. Ringing sound from clan *golf* (5)

19. Crazily, let native **aerate** (9)

21. Tavern gained from winnings (3)

22. Unsteadily exert with me — it's **intense!** (7)

23. Drunk Snaky **pulls!** (5)

Down

1. Maniac cut nail badly (7)

2. Abdominal pain from bleach and lye mixture (9)

3. Dreadful sleet at **American city** (7)

4. Insane captain's moose is **sympathetic** (13)

5. Badger lost its tail for **an emblem** (5)

6. Pointed tool found in bandsaw lesson (3)

7. *Queen* has lyric poem revealing **decay** (5)

12. Iota Man in mad **movie technique** (9)

14. Smashed a cherry for **sport** (7)

15. Tales of limb ends (7)

16. *One* in action **film** (5)

17. Wrap *model* alcoholic drink (5)

20. Almond, perhaps, discovered amongst minutiae (3)

Puzzle 7

Across

1. Commercial corruption **guidance** (6)

4. Vigorous *turkey* engaged in song (6)

8. Bahutu xenophile has a **short dinner jacket** (3)

9. Nude has a *grand* **elbow** (5)

11. Teak cut short yields **oolong, perhaps**? (3)

12. Cross-questioning one rioting rat, after a fashion (13)

15. Malamute is half **tongue-tied** (4)

16. Marine mammal's emblem (4)

20. Deranged capital morons make **official announcements** (13)

21. Little devil is seen in denim pants (3)

23. Mixed *carbon* into **restorative drink** (5)

24. Noisily produce an egg for a **flower garland** (3)

25. Ed Grey absurdly **grasping** (6)

26. Banner on **wine jug** (6)

Down

1. Secure a Titan, struggling (6)

2. Annoy, and send up in a hoax event (3)

3. Praised shivering cold great-aunt (13)

5. Spurious peace and truth ail **healing** (13)

6. Pick *circuit physical training* (3)

7. *Good* showers for **cereals** (6)

10. Physician lacking heart for **an entrance** (4)

13. Speed of crazy *master* poet (5)

14. Erroneously go oil the **Inuit house** (5)

17. Season elastic coil (6)

18. Portent from topless ladies (4)

19. Allocate snags I cooked (6)

22. Regularly price **a baked treat** (3)

24. Member knocked over gel (3)

Puzzle 8

Across

1. It's **demoralising**, heeding strain badly (13)

8. Unbind Auntie — she lost her head! (5)

9. Island *saint* left acrostics in a mess (7)

10. I hear 'Chop down **shade**!' (3)

11. Greek philosopher totes lira around (9)

13. Artist's supports, as in eels (6)

14. Billy *Good* is distraught, **shallowly** (6)

17. Cunning Sisi in duo screwed up (9)

19. Mythological bird? Endless crock! (3)

20. Graceful twisted moss lei (7)

22. Bulb on charged particle (5)

23. Whine? Hoot? Pine? Naughty **Piglet's pal**! (6,3,4)

Down

1. Son's wife's dual nightwear is disarrayed (8-2-3)

2. Rest? It's disturbed for **child minders** (7)

3. Stared at intoxicated Lady Beele (9)

4. Jump back *about* loop (6)

5. Better report contains **blunder** (3)

6. Mild ricotta evenly covers **halfwit** (5)

7. Small purple lily discovered by mad teaching harpy (5,8)

12. Scientific instrument *company* put inside a broken steeple (9)

15. Tortilla wrap? A small donkey consumes it (7)

16. Secret is over in *Connecticut* (6)

18. Sarandon spotted in Pegasus animation (5)

21. Sash *Duck vitamin* (3)

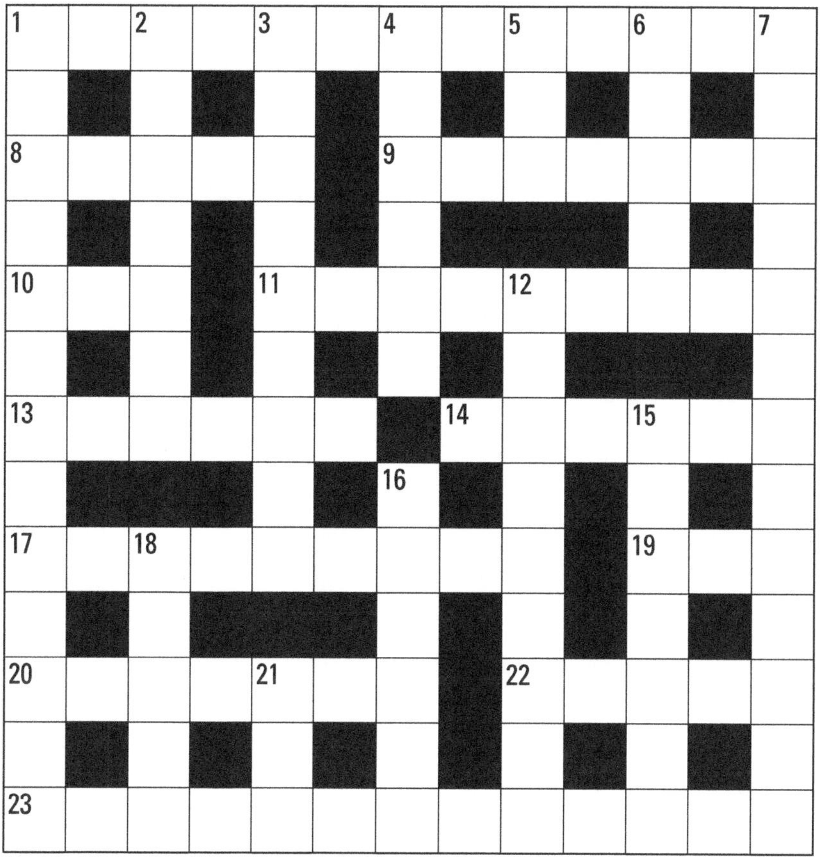

Chapter **13**
Challenging Cryptics

I n this chapter there are four medium crosswords for you to work on. There are several ways I've made these crosswords a bit easier than 'regular' cryptics.

As with the easy crosswords in Chapter 12, the grids are smaller than a regular crossword, only 13 × 13 squares; each puzzle has about 30 clues.

There are no extremely rare or hard words, but my vocabulary choices are wider than those in the easy crosswords — you might need to check a dictionary occasionally for a definition or a place name.

There are still more anagram and hidden word clues than you see in a newspaper cryptic, but fewer than were in the easy crosswords. Quite a few words are 'in clear view' within the wordplay, too.

I give you hints with every clue. Any words that lead to abbreviations are set in *italics*. Any indicator words in a clue are set in **bold**. This will help you figure out what sort of cryptic device is being used. It also helps you narrow down which part of the clue is the definition. Clues that don't have any indicator words are generally charade or double definition clues.

So, without further ado . . . grab your pencil and turn the page!

Puzzle 9

Across

4. Can **rotate** the pen point? (3)

7. **Sadly** abide act, and renounce throne (8)

8. Check *about one Pole* (4)

9. Red snail **crushed** for Fijian, perhaps (8)

10. Ha! To **destroy** a solemn promise (4)

11. Baby cat knit **busily** with *alien* (6)

14. Cowardly, shout an exclamation of pain! (6)

15. Terrified *answer* to *loud* raid (6)

17. Run, **hugging** *nickel* pastry (6)

19. German composer's **half** a bachelor (4)

20. **Unusual** red opals for big cats (8)

23. Divide a hot drink with *Romeo* (4)

24. **Deranged** relation is from Asia (8)

25. Simpleton *son* to *answer softly* (3)

Down

1. Wading bird's **leaders absent from** legal defences (4)

2. Celebrated soprano **brought up** eager (4)

3. **Crazy** gander makes a flower bed (6)

4. *Bridge player* ahead of time, almost (6)

5. Lyn after creek for New York borough (8)

6. **Uncontrolled** virus out — it's morally correct (8)

9. **Short** mink's writing medium (3)

12. **Whipped** fine salt blows up (8)

13. Lecturers **shaking** cheaters (8)

16. Blob's model *operation* (6)

17. Bondi ox innocently **shows** poison (6)

18. Possessive **part of** anarchist (3)

21. A uni **mix-up** for the Japanese native (4)

22. *Daughter* rodent's exclamation! (4)

Puzzle 10

Across

1. Pass over, angry (5)

4. Babies in fan t-shirts, **to some extent** (7)

8. Singer **missing lead** is a dolt (3)

9. Untreatable? Expose self to expert (9)

10. Weird briny lath maze (9)

12. *Vermont* **accepting** a tank (3)

13. Craftily cite usual ploy to get some natural antiseptic (10,3)

15. Also **found in** tomato omelette (3)

16. *Credit* **in chopped** aconite growth (9)

17. Small marsupial robber **adopts** dove's sound (9)

20. Sick tablet **initially lost** (3)

21. Comes out to see germ **transforming** (7)

22. Flying mammal on musical wand (5)

Down

1. Scorch Whopper for chocolate factory heir (7)

2. Coco sub so **cooked**, it makes an Italian dish (9)

3. Travel over snow, and **almost** miss out (3)

4. Unobtrusive but **fishy** innocuous pics (13)

5. Chaotic hour's fame in rural home (9)

6. Core bread roll **turnover** (3)

7. Perfume posted **by air** (5)

11. Delivering **broken** easel **found in** ring (9)

12. One who plays **types of** viol in Istanbul (9)

14. Mix-up in *student* loan for wool fat (7)

15. Buffet *bachelor* **in** story (5)

18. Odd niece's original name (3)

19. Instrument **cut short** to make a container (3)

Puzzle 11

Across

1. Placates with *100* handouts to the poor (5)

5. Ebbs and flows, diets **all at sea** (5)

8. Greeting *left* in **crooked** hole (5)

9. Odd *graduate* dance (5)

10. Relative is unclear, **missing finals** (5)

11. Sink vapour **flows backwards** (3)

12. Knock *King Oklahoma* to Thai capital (7)

16. Head off virginal impetuosity (5)

18. Put together a young woman, **by the sound of it** (4)

20. Help Di **rearrange** the Oracle's home (6)

22. Busy *northern* local is ready for work at any time (2,4)

24. A male cat's particle (4)

26. Woman **seen in both directions** (5)

28. Darling vole **turned over in** bed (7)

32. Gibson's **half of a** song (3)

33. Monk's room has *old* instrument (5)

34. Argon **swirled** into lung, perhaps (5)

35. *Carbon* becomes old pens (5)

36. Beat whiskers **without** hesitations (5)

37. Em in *eastern New York* is no friend (5)

Down

1. Inebriated cobra makes St John's Bread (5)

2. Len **carries** Mo to crap car (5)

3. *Sierra*, listen! It's a marine predator! (5)

4. State **part of** approval as karaoke (6)

5. Beef up one thug **at random** (7)

6. Decorates ship's floors (5)

7. Reportedly noticed landscape (5)

13. A *King* Beer tipped over Cub Scout leader (5)

14. Pause, agape, **missing outsiders** (3)

15. Exclude **from** classroom itinerary (4)

17. Net **decapitated** mullet, **crushed** (5)

19. Vault demo **broken up** (4)

21. Hack mom **made up** bed (7)

23. Tailless coot makes a dove's sound (3)

25. Do a favour, **remarkably** glib in *Old English* (6)

26. Large parrot with *Massachusetts* Crow's cry (5)

27. Indian city's specialty food store **announced** (5)

29. Be defeated, **grasping** *nothing* wobbly (5)

30. *Very* old fever is ill-defined (5)

31. Glamour boy **concealed in** cummerbund and y-fronts (5)

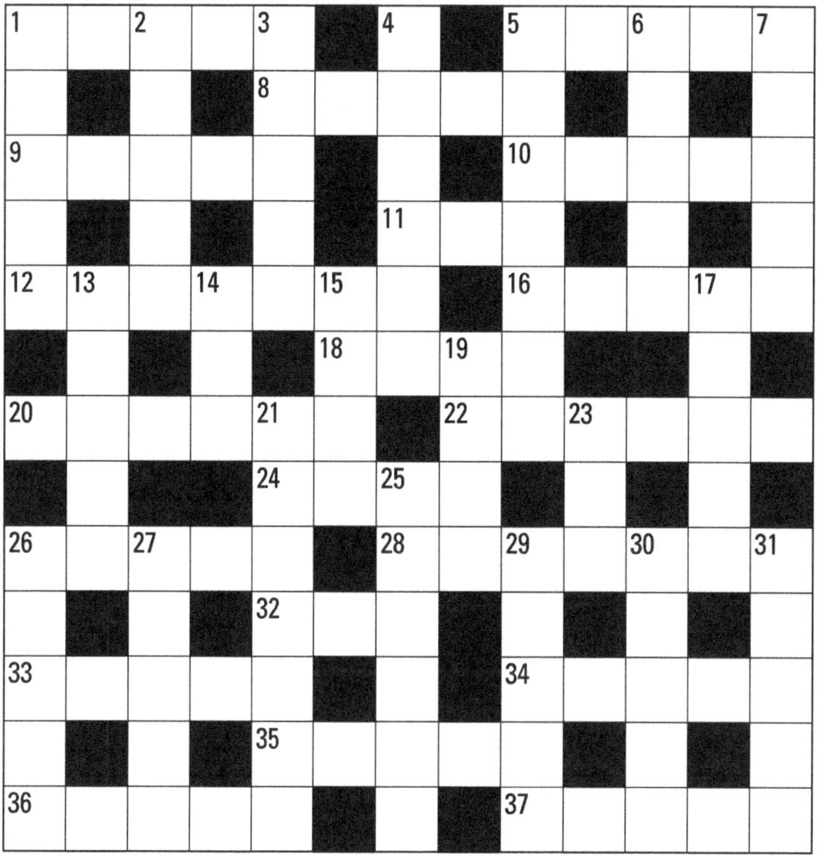

Puzzle 12

Across

1. *Bachelor* Con has tasty accompaniment for eggs (5)

4. Pastries' calories **lose** *nothing*, **unexpectedly!** (7)

8. West Indies' bare cabin **is smashed up** (9)

9. Part of boat **passing over** *king* fish (3)

10. Follow *in French*, Sue (5)

11. Congestion results if craft **gets damaged** (7)

13. Horrific continual hail brings on a vision (13)

15. A dog is **central to** Christmas tiff (7)

16. Disaster **set back** *soprano*'s emotional states (5)

18. Rocky peak's deterioration **reversed** (3)

20. Highly unpleasant *old boy* with no *variable promises to pay* (9)

21. Never **return** to *good bridge player* for vengeance (7)

22. Dangerous *Rhode Island* atmosphere (5)

Down

1. *Bowled nothing* with *Charlie* before *this French* Italian game (5)

2. Butterfly pupa has lyrics, **strangely** (9)

3. Broken *left* bone is elevated (5)

4. Dizzily flee eccentric charged barrier (8,5)

5. Lana **hugs** *worker* providing weed (7)

6. Mike **lost his head** for Eisenhower (3)

7. Element **damaged** *the Italian* coins (7)

12. Silly **jazzy** viol for us (9)

13. European rodent coming from bad actors' *territory* (7)

14. *One French island* has maize for mythical horse (7)

16. *Unknown* Emir **crazy** for soft drink (5)

17. Effeminate Chris is sympathetic, **in part** (5)

19. Edit **half** for short priest (3)

Chapter **14**

Treacherous Cryptics

his chapter has four hard crosswords for you to try out. Don't be too daunted, though, there are hints for every crossword in Chapter 15, and you can always have a peek at the answers in Chapter 16 if you're really stuck.

The crosswords in this chapter are very similar to what you're likely to find in a newspaper cryptic crossword. I haven't restricted the vocabulary in the crosswords or the clues, and the grids are of normal size (15 × 15).

There are some less common words both in the grids and the clues, so you are more likely to need to check in a dictionary or thesaurus with these puzzles.

There are still a few more anagram clues than you'd find in a hard cryptic from a newspaper, but fewer than in the easy and medium crosswords in this book. Some words are 'in the clear' (you don't need to find a synonym for them), but not that many. You'll see more charade clues, and clues that use several cryptic devices in combination.

There are no hints in these puzzles, no indications of which words are definitions or indicators, or lead to abbreviations. Keep in mind that any given word can be part of the definition, an indicator word, an abbreviation, or another part of the wordplay! Also remember that abbreviations are used widely in cryptic clues; there is a good list of them in the Appendix.

Two of the grids in this chapter have designs whereby you don't get as many initial letters for the crossing over words; for these puzzles I have provided extra hints in Chapter 15, to help you along the way.

Puzzle 13

Across

1. Sat back during passing over a small cup of coffee (9)

6. Pro gets no good tip (5)

9. Reversed circuit for a friend (3)

10. Unfortunate rebel target suffering demolition (11)

11. Fulfil longing for one outstanding in their field (5)

12. Have guests come in, thanks, at home (9)

14. Crumbed fried rolls? Lose three at the end of the game (7)

15. Salvage vitamin in chopped celery (7)

17. Ineptly derails, and rings again (7)

19. Insulting, without model George's hormone (7)

20. Oh! Eve bent out of shape composer (9)

22. See eye to eye, deliriously eager (5)

24. Irritated past lover separated horribly (11)

26. Pull belly around (3)

27. Put it in a dot accidentally — it's the same thing again (5)

28. Vaguely re-did apse and lost hope (9)

Down

1. Sulked — swap Mike for daughter given drugs (5)

2. Pamper spoilt model coldly (11)

3. Large spider is natural at juggling (9)

4. Get a bit from, say, fellows in the street (7)

5. Voter let core explode (7)

6. Ustinov's confused expert missing a kiss (5)

7. Seen within absorbent sphere (3)

8. Haphazard northern bee range produces vegetable (5,4)

13. Performer eats cereal, mashed with car's pedal (11)

14. British sailors in brocade mixed up American side dish (9)

16. Trojan princess darns a sac poorly (9)

18. Badly deserve to be cut off (7)

19. Carelessly, I ingest lights (7)

21. Fashionable post office represents mammal (5)

23. Bordered and sprinkled with sugar, dismissing the doctor (5)

25. Even strands of carpets are relevant (3)

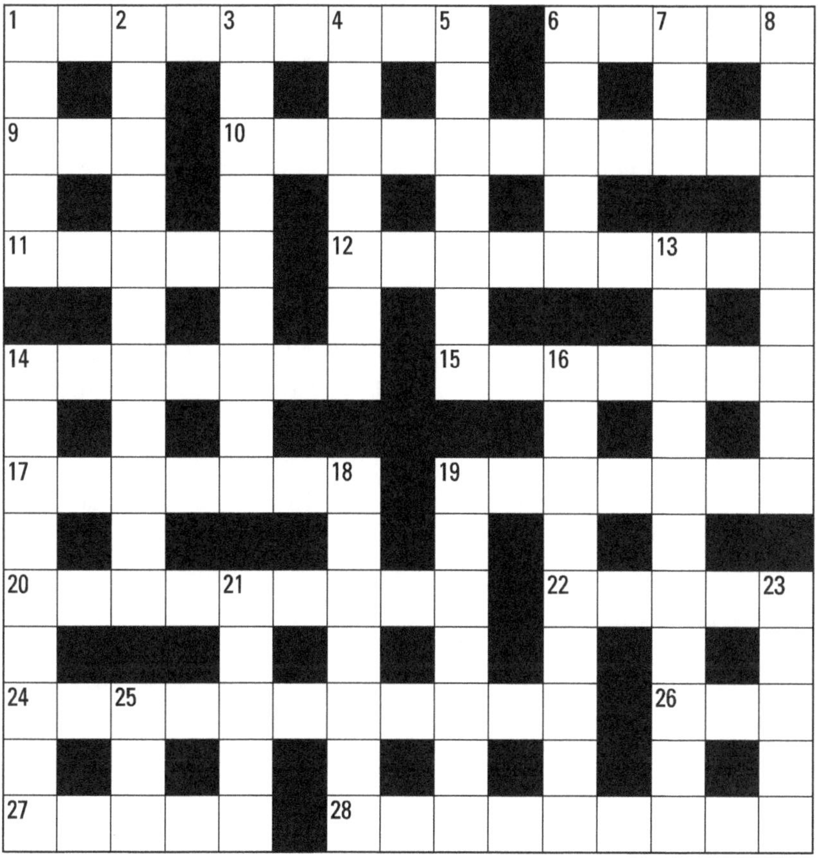
1 2 3 4 5 6 7 8
9 10
11 12 13
14 15 16
17 18 19
20 21 22 23
24 25 26
27 28

Puzzle 14

Note: The sort of grid design used in this puzzle (which you find in cryptics elsewhere) is harder, because the crossing over words don't provide as many initial letters. Because of this, I have provided more hints for this crossword in Chapter 15.

Across

8. Rubbish ban due for a German river (6)

9. Big ship with eastern gifts (8)

10. Roughly eject divas for describing words (10)

11. Exhaled, depressed, so to speak (4)

12. Float, ill at sea with small fleet (8)

14. Work up trouble, in quote (6)

15. Unruly baritone demands gambling machines (3-5,7)

18. Takeover circuit with new discount voucher (6)

20. Forced, one leaves millipede, upset (8)

22. Glass container is dreadful, I've heard (4)

23. Chance to delight in Long Island cowl (10)

25. Tiny creatures board a heavy weight (8)

26. Help back, in tavern from Mumbai (6)

Down

1. Musical instrument slicer (8)

2. Edict is cerulean, in part (4)

3. Badly tend Albert of the Teeth (6)

4. Viking lad in cake mixture is vigorously doing well (5,3,7)

5. Orchestral section — one about cabbage, perhaps? (8)

6. Fermented Chili Bread is fatal to plants (10)

7. Insist on synthetic asters (6)

13. Stomp over the bar with acrobatic equipment (10)

16. Scattered moonlight missing German menhir (8)

17. On the wagon, with golf peg complete (8)

19. Otherwise, I ring the French American blackbird? (6)

21. Dad has herb coming up, pale and sickly (6)

24. Camouflage the tanned skin (4)

Puzzle 15

Across

1. Drone on one day, it's muggy (5)

4. Reversible storm tracker (5)

7. Dump the gratuity (3)

9. Disorderly colonel is guided to an apple (6,9)

10. Having an operation on Tuesday? I'm a supporter, ideally (9)

11. Patter and run in Roman robe, looking backwards (5)

12. Protest against fermented hive gin (7)

14. Stag got around, encountered Persephone's mum (7)

16. Put up the money for nitrogen and sulphur to be put into animal's scent (7)

18. Correct Scarlet concerning the steamship (7)

19. G'day! King Edward went by foot (5)

20. A melange of ripe pâtés for the first course (9)

22. Ending correspondence abused elder Jean's troth (4,4,7)

24. Note tucked in camisole (3)

25. Pour fat over glue, bravo for Papa! (5)

26. A backwards stance for fable teller (5)

Down

1. Embrace the gangster, who's missing his leader (3)

2. Foolish to omit oval clock of crude explosive (7,8)

3. Fantasy mare has 500 bananas (5)

4. Crazed upholder lost eastern red-nosed one (7)

5. The Italian unknown infiltrated brave feat, and was detained (7)

6. Request involved in swamp plan being saved (9)

7. Showing lack of consideration, hushes Glen's tots improperly (15)

8. Pole includes one, and set forth (5)

10. Shuts out and throws up, missing the start (5)

13. Join Debi's nasty crime, committed by a worker (6,3)

15. Sir backs up with hesitation for one who gets out of bed (5)

17. Stretches out and hurts again? (7)

18. Disgust about chickpea, perhaps (7)

19. Scolds, loses head, and takes cover (5)

21. Turkey tucked into a hot drink and a little fish (5)

23. Oddly slurp and eat dinner (3)

Puzzle 16

Note: Because of the grid design used in this puzzle, which doesn't provide many initial letters, I provide more hints for you for this puzzle in Chapter 15.

Across

7. Broken torch housing over unit (6)

9. Playing Ghana, amid archaic lonely and abandoned cattle breed (8)

10. Floppy hobble (4)

11. Meeting requirements to destroy quay filing (10)

12. Mexican stew made with niche lilac corn, chopped up (6,3,5)

15. Italian sparkling wine feature of tasting (4)

16. Violin-making family is first class, including Mat (5)

17. Greek letter repeated to tasty mollusc (4)

19. Busily tweet using sort of tricksy texts (6-8)

20. Glass slipper lass harassed lid cleaner (10)

23. Neat feature of literati dynasty (4)

24. In retrospect, scrap Rhode Island son's regiment (8)

25. The Spanish six hush, impish (6)

Down

1. Is he in rising waste water with varnishes? (8)

2. Obsession with up-lions.com, strangely (10)

3. University student with sodium and a bone (4)

4. Mad Mini's dire antic is done at random (14)

5. Sounds like a method to get something from milk (4)

6. Third prize model, instead of Zulu English author? (6)

8. Orange cocktail from blended liqueur nasties (7,7)

13. Abstract movement round section (2,3)

14. Routine is erratically interpretive, ignoring the English sailors (10)

18. Grand procession around island idyll (8)

19. A Twain went to pieces, representing an Asian island (6)

21. Black argon in Denmark (4)

22. Heather fish (4)

Hints and Answers

This part is where I reveal all! Here, I provide hints and answers to all the puzzles from Part 2.

First, I give you some help if you're a bit stuck on a crossword, in the form of hints to some of the clues. This should help you get a few answers worked out. Do see if these hints can help you out first before sneaking a look at the answers chapter. Once you have a few words in the grid, you're likely to find cracking the other clues easier.

Then, if you want to check your answers or are really stuck, have a look at Chapter 16, which has all the answers to all the crosswords in Part 2.

Chapter **15**
Hints

I n this chapter, I give you at least ten hints for each of the Part 2 crosswords. I'd love to be sitting next to you and helping you out, but clearly that's rather impractical, so hopefully these little whispers from me are enough to give you more of a foothold on each crossword.

Getting a Helping Hand

In the following section, I provide hints for the easy crosswords in Chapter 12, the medium-level crosswords in Chapter 13 and the hard crosswords in Chapter 14.

So have a look in these sections first, before resorting to the answers. But if you're still really stuck, by all means check out the answers in Chapter 16!

Chapter 12: Easy Peasy Cryptics

Crossword 1

Across: 1. *Holds* is a hidden word indicator 9. *Noisily* is a homophone indicator 13. *Out* is an anagram indicator 19. *Shows us* is indicating a hidden word clue 20. The answer starts with T

Down: 1. This is a charade clue 3. *Discovered in* indicates a hidden word clue 6. *Improperly* is an anagram indicator 14. *Swallow* is a verb, not a bird 21. *Rodents* are MICE

Crossword 2

Across: 1. *Tipped over* is an anagram indicator 7. *Oddly* means to look at the odd-numbered letters in another part of the clue 20. An anagram of *gold* (AU) and STAIR 23. This is a double definition clue 28. *Disguises* = MASKS

Down: 6. *Run away* can be to FLEE 13. A *line* = QUEUE 15. This is a double definition clue 19. The word *our* appears in plain view and doesn't need a synonym 21. The *note* in question here is FA

Crossword 3

Across: 1. The answer starts with I 14. A double definition clue 16. *Announced* indicates a homophone clue 23. *Among* is a container indicator 26. *On radio* indicates a homophone clue

Down: 3. A double definition clue 5. *Converted* is an anagram indicator 6. *Article* = AN (indefinite article) 15. *XXX* = THIRTY 19. *Hiding* is a hidden word indicator

Crossword 4

Across: 6. This is a double definition clue 9. *Chilly* = COLD and *ship* = SS 16. The answer starts with IN 24. The answer starts with CL 27. *Odd* tells you to look at the odd-numbered letters in the wordplay

Down: 3. Scottish hat = TAM 4. *About* = C (from *circa*) 12. *Almost* means to remove a letter from *singer* 19. *Contain* indicates a hidden word clue 21. *Small lobsters* = SCAMPI

Crossword 5

Across: 3. Hidden word clue 11. The answer starts with TR 14. *Duck* = O 18. *Phoney* is an anagram indicator 24. *Jazzy* is an anagram indicator

Down: 2. *Greek letter* = MU 3. The answer starts with DI 8. *Mutant* is an anagram indicator and the answer starts with I 16. *Unusual* indicates an anagram 19. *Perhaps* means that *lead* is an example of the answer

Crossword 6

Across: 1. *Exist* = BE 9. *Funny* is an anagram indicator 13. The answer beings with CO 16. The answer starts with M 19. The answer starts with V

Down: 2. *Mixture* is an anagram indicator 4. The answer starts with CO 7. *Queen* is abbreviated here as ER 15. This is a charade clue 17. *Model* is abbreviated as T (Model T Ford)

Crossword 7

Across: 1. *Corruption* = VICE 4. *Turkey* (the country, not the bird!) is abbreviated as TR 12. The answer starts with IN 20. *Deranged* is an anagram indicator 26. *Banner* = FLAG

Down: 2. *Send up in* indicates a reversed hidden word 3. The answer starts with CO 5. *Spurious* is an anagram indicator 10. *Lacking heart* means to remove the middle letters of another word for *physician* 22. *Regularly* indicates to look at alternate letter positions in the word *price*

Crossword 8

Across: 1. An anagram clue, the answer starts with DIS 11. *Around* is an anagram indicator 13. This is a container clue, put AS into EELS 19. *Endless* means to delete the first and last letters off the word *crock* 23. *Naughty* is an anagram indicator

Down: 1. The answer starts with DA 2. Ignore the punctuation! *Disturbed* is an anagram indicator 6. *Evenly* means to look at the even letters in the words *mild ricotta* 15. *A small donkey* = BURRO 21. *Vitamin* = BI (for Vitamin B1) in this clue

Chapter 13: Challenging Cryptics

Crossword 9

Across: 8. *About* = RE 11. *Alien* = ET 14. An *exclamation of pain* = OW (of course!) 17. *Run* = DASH 24. *Deranged* is an anagram indicator

Down: 2. *Brought up* is a reversal indicator 5. The answer starts with B 12. The answer starts with IN 16. *Model* = DOLL 17. This is a hidden word clue

Crossword 10

Across: 8. *Singer* = BASS in this clue 13. The answer starts with EU 15. *Also* is the definition 17. *Adopts* is a container indicator 22. *Musical wand* is the definition in this charade clue

Down: 1. Think of a Roald Dahl story! 4. The answer starts with INC 6. *Turnover* is a reversal indicator 7. This is a homophone clue 15. *Buffet* (as a noun) is the definition

Crossword 11

Across: 1. *Handouts to the poor* are ALMS 9. *Odd* = RUM 16. *Virginal* = CHASTE 32. *Song* = MELODY 35. *Becomes old* = AGES 36. *Hesitations* = ERS

Down: 1. The answer starts with C 3. This is a charade clue (and not a homophone!) 6. This is a double definition clue 14. *Missing outsiders* means to remove the start and end letters 30. An *old fever* is an AGUE (an old-fashioned word for a fever)

Crossword 12

Across: 4. *Lose nothing* means to delete the letter O from *calories* 9. *Passing over* is a deletion indicator 13. The answer starts with HA 15. This is a hidden word clue 20. *Promises to pay* are IOUS

Down: 1. *Bowled* = B (a cricket term) in this charade clue 4. The answer starts with EL and *dizzily* is an anagram indicator 12. *Silly* is the definition 13. *Bad actors* = HAMS in this charade clue 19. *Edit* = REVISE and the definition is a *short* form of a word for a *priest*

Chapter 14: Treacherous Cryptics

Crossword 13

Across: 1. *Passing over* = DEMISE 6. *Tip* is the definition 14. *Crumbed fried rolls* = CROQUETTES 19. *Model* = T (Model T Ford) 27. The answer starts with D

Down: 1. This is a substitution clue, so you need to swap one letter for another, and *sulked* = MOPED 2. *Spoilt* is an anagram indicator 3. *Juggling* indicates an anagram 6. *Kiss* = X 13. *Performer* = ACTOR 14. *British sailors* = RN (for Royal Navy)

Crossword 14

Across: 8. *Rubbish* is an anagram indicator 9. *Ship* = SS and the answer starts with L 12. *At sea* indicates an anagram 15. *Unruly* is an anagram indicator 18. *Takeover* = COUP 20. *One* = I and you need to take it out of *millipede* 22. *Dreadful* = VILE 25. *Tiny creatures* is the definition

Down: 1. A double definition clue, starting with M 3. *Albert* = AL 5. *Cabbage, perhaps* is the definition and *about* = CA (circa) 6. *Fermented* is an anagram indicator 13. *Stomp* = TRAMP and *over* = O (cricketing abbreviation) 16. *German* = G 24. A double definition clue

Crossword 15

Across: 1. *Drone* = HUM 4. A palindrome! 11. *Run* = R (cricket) and *Roman robe* = TOGA 14. *Encountered* = MET 16. *Animal's scent* = SPOOR 22. The words of the answer start with D, J and L

Down: 2. The answer words start with M and C 3. *Bananas* is an anagram indicator 6. *Request* = CLAIM and *saved* is the definition 8. *Pole* = POST 17. This clue delves into a little 'language abuse' with *hurts again* (that is, it's not a dictionary definition!) 21. *Turkey* = TR

Crossword 16

Across: 7. *Unit* is the definition and *housing* is a container indicator 9. An *archaic* word for *lonely and abandoned* is LORN 15. A hidden word clue, indicated by *feature of* 16. *First class* = AI (A1) 17. The *Greek letter* in question here is PI 19. The two words in the answer both start with T 24. A *scrap* is a RAG and it needs to be read backwards (*in retrospect*)

Down: 1. *Waste water* = SLOP 4. *Done at random* is the definition 5. A homophone clue, indicated by *sounds like* 6. A substitution clue, *English author* is the definition 8. The answer words start with T and S 13. A *section* is a PART and *movement* is not an anagram indicator here! 18. *Idyll* is the definition 21. *Denmark* = DK

Chapter **16**
Answers

Chapter 12: Easy Peasy Cryptics

Puzzle 1

Puzzle 2

Puzzle 3

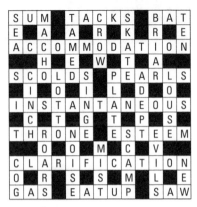

Puzzle 4

Puzzle 5

Puzzle 6

Puzzle 7

Puzzle 8

Chapter 13: Challenging Cryptics

Puzzle 9

Puzzle 10

Puzzle 11

Puzzle 12

Chapter 14: Treacherous Cryptics

Puzzle 13

Puzzle 14

Puzzle 15

Puzzle 16

4

The Part of Tens

In this part, I provide some useful extras. First, I give you my top ten tips on how to be a better solver of cryptics, so you can gradually hone your skills. I then provide a list of cryptic crossword resources. These are handy books, websites and apps that can help you when you're stuck, as well as some websites that have good collections of free cryptic crosswords you might like to work your way up to.

The Appendix has some great lists, which I hope you refer to often when solving cryptics! I provide a list of common cryptic indicator words, a list of the most commonly seen foreign words used in cryptics and a good basic list of cryptic abbreviations.

Chapter **17**

Ten Tips for Being a Better Solver

S o, you've got the cryptic crossword bug (sorry, no known cure exists)! This book is just a basic introduction to this perplexing genre and the crosswords here are only from one setter (yours truly!). So, what can you do to expand your horizons and become an even more expert solver? In this chapter, I outline my top ten tips for improving your game.

Practising and Practising — then Practising Some More

Practise, practise, practise! Trust me — you really can get better with practice. Even if you can only get out two clues in a newspaper crossword now, that's still two clues! Good job! And next week you might get four clues. You gradually get to know the setter's style and doing so helps with your clue solving.

If you're serious about improving your cryptic solving skills, I suggest attempting to solve one crossword per day. If you're less obsessed but still want to make progress, aim to work on one or two crosswords per week.

REMEMBER

One of the reasons cryptic crosswords hold such an attraction for so many people is that they're challenging and hard; even when you're an experienced solver, some clues can really perplex you. So, please don't feel badly if you can't get every clue!

Cheating Just a Bit

Don't be afraid to 'cheat' (just as long as you're not in a competition setting!). I actually think it's a fantastic learning method — try your best to get the clues out but, if you're stuck on some words, take a peek at the answers at the back of the book, use the 'reveal a word' function if solving a cryptic online, or wait for the answer to be printed in the newspaper.

Find out what the answer to the troublesome clue is. See if you can work backwards from the answer. Identify the definition part of the clue. Can you figure out how the wordplay works? Are abbreviations used in the clue? Or indicator words?

You may also like to use solving aids to help you get answers when you're stuck — in this case, see Chapter 18 for my recommendations. These often present you with a selection of words that fit that particular letter pattern in the grid, and then you can see if you can find the answer from the resulting list.

Knowing What It Doesn't Mean

As soon as you read any cryptic clue, you can tell exactly what it *doesn't* mean right away! The 'surface reading' — the mental image you get when reading the clue 'as is' — is only meant to distract and confuse you. So, from the very start, discount the surface reading and start looking under the surface, for what the clue is *really* telling you!

Only in a few rare clue types (*&lit* and *cryptic definitions* — refer to Chapter 11) does the surface reading actually have a bearing on the clue.

Looking for Alternatives and Patterns

Remember that any given word may have quite a few possible meanings. As one example, look at the word *around*. Within a cryptic clue, this single word can be:

>> An **abbreviation**, leading to C or CA (for *circa*)

>> A **container indicator**, indicating that you need to put one word *around* another one

>> A **reversal indicator**, telling you to turn a word *around* the other way

>> A **definition**, for words like *everywhere, nearby, surrounding* or *roughly*; it can be defined as an adverb or a preposition

>> A **synonym** for another word, which is used in the wordplay

>> **Anagram 'fodder'**, forming a part of ROTUNDAS, perhaps!

REMEMBER

Reading each word in a clue with an eye to multiple meanings, parts of speech and functions with the clue is very important — this is really the key to cracking cryptics.

Also look for patterns in the grid and examine any part answers. The beauty of crosswords as puzzles is that each time you get one word into the grid, you get letters for the crossing-over words! For example, words ending with a D most probably end in RD or ED; if the last letter is a G, the last three letters are most likely ING. Looking at common letter patterns like this can help you add more letters to the grid, even if you can't get the clue out.

Spotting Unusual Sorts of Clues

While you may well attest that all cryptic clues are unusual (yeah, actually, you've got a point there), most clues in a standard cryptic crossword fall into the various cryptic devices that I explain in Part 1 of this book.

However, occasionally, other less common clue devices are used, so you need to be on the lookout for these. Less common clue devices such as substitution clues (where one letter is substituted for another) and Libertarian clue devices do crop up now and then! Refer to Chapter 11 for more on this.

Learn to read a clue for what it means and to follow the setter's 'instructions', even if the clue device doesn't appear to fit into a set clue device that you're used to — this can help you get by any of the less common devices. And if a clue really stumps you, don't feel too bad — it has no doubt confused many other solvers as well!

Getting Away from It All

Here's a tried and true method — letting your unconscious brain do the hard work while you sleep! If you're really getting nowhere with a crossword, and just feeling frustrated and aggravated, have a break. You don't have any deadlines (at least, I hope not!), and solving a cryptic is supposed to be fun, after all. Come back to the puzzle after a few hours, or the next day. You may be surprised at how often this break is all you need — suddenly that intractable clue becomes amazingly obvious!

Memorising Lists

Familiarise yourself with the lists of abbreviations used in cryptics, as well as the foreign words (see the Appendix for more on these) and things like short river names (such as OB, PO, EXE, DEE and ORD) which often crop up in cryptic crosswords. As you gain more experience with solving cryptics, these become second nature to you, too.

Choosing Your Setters

Get used to the work of one or two cryptic setters at a time; be aware that different setters write clues slightly differently and that different newspapers and publishers have different rules and standards for cryptic clues.

When you can comfortably solve the cryptics by a few setters, start to expand your horizons, and try harder cryptics. Get to know who is regarded as hard (for example, Arucaria) and easier (for example, Rufus) among the UK setters, in particular.

Building Your Vocabulary

Expanding your vocabulary is a great way to improve your skills at cryptic crosswords — in fact, solving cryptics naturally expands your vocabulary, too! Many books, websites and software programs can help you improve your vocabulary. You may like to check out my website `english-language-skills.com` or `www.vocabulary.com`.

You can also subscribe to one of the many 'Word of the Day' emails. The following websites are just a few examples of sites that offer this free service:

>> Dictionary.com (dictionary.reference.com)

>> Oxford English Dictionary (`www.oed.com`)

>> The Free Dictionary (`www.thefreedictionary.com`)

Getting Involved Online

A host of online resources, blogs and crossword clubs are available, including the Australian Crossword Club (`www.crosswordclub.org`) and British Crossword Club (`www.thecrosswordclub.co.uk`), and both focus on cryptics.

Some good solving blogs are also available online, where daily crosswords (generally from the UK papers) are dissected and each clue explained.

You may like to visit:

- >> Crossword Unclued: www.crosswordunclued.com
- >> Fifteensquared: fifteensquared.net
- >> Sutherland Studios: sutherland-studios.com.au/blog (my blog)

Of course, many other cryptic blogs are written by both setters and solvers (being a rather wordy bunch!). The websites listed include many links that can lead you to other blogs.

Chapter **18**
Ten (Plus Two!) Puzzling Resources

This chapter contains some of my favourite solving resources, starting with books and then moving on to websites and apps. Search for the apps in the app store, via your mobile device, or visit the programmers' websites, listed in the relevant sections in this chapter, for more information. I also give you a bonus resource — albeit one that's a book that's now out of print, so a little more difficult to find.

I often use these resources when setting my cryptics, and I hope that you find some of them useful too!

TIP

Before getting stuck into this chapter, it's a good idea to have some understanding of what *wildcard searches* are. This term is often used in crossword solver websites and apps. In cards, a wildcard is a card that can be assigned any value, colour, suit or other property by the player. Similarly, in computing terminology, it's a character that can equal any character. Say you're stumped on a clue but have a few checked letters in the grid, giving you the entry 'D-something-U-something-something'. What you need to do is a 'wildcard search' — each 'something' becomes a wildcard search character, often using an asterisk, question mark or a full stop (period). So, you type 'D*U**' into the search box and you're given all the options for words that fit that pattern (25 words, including DEUCE, DOUBT, DOUGH and DRUMS, in this case). As you can see, with this sort of wildcard search, the asterisks can equal any letter from A to Z.

Chambers Crossword Dictionary

The Chambers reference books in general are the best for crossword solvers (and setters!), and provide help with solving both cryptic and quick crosswords. Chambers have dedicated themselves to producing reference works that have been used by puzzle solvers and setters for decades, and this dedication shows!

This huge dictionary, edited by Elaine Higgleton and Catherine Schwarz, is up to its fourth edition (published in 2015) and has over 500,000 entries. It lists over 2,500 indicator words, as well as a wealth of anagrams, words arranged by category and listed by length, cryptic abbreviations and homophones. It also includes advice on solving cryptic crosswords from some of the British cryptic crossword greats.

Bradford's Crossword Solver's Dictionary

This book by Anne R. Bradford (10th Edition published in 2016) is a great resource for solving quick and cryptic crosswords. It includes huge lists of synonyms for various key words (such as a five-page list of every bird name imaginable, arranged by letter length), as well as synonyms for more unusual words. Also covered are cryptic abbreviations and cryptic indicators.

The words following each keyword entry can include synonyms, associated adjectives, associated or proper nouns, and any puns or devious plays on words associated with that keyword.

Cryptic Crossword Solver: An Out-of-Print Gem

This slender paperback by Jennifer Chandler (published in 1991) is one of my favourite reference books, so even though it's now out of print, I still think it's useful to include here — and well worth the effort to search for. It's Australian and has pretty much all the basic information you need when solving cryptic crosswords.

Included in the book is a very concise, handy list of commonly used abbreviations, foreign words, homophones and definitions used in cryptic crosswords, and common indicator words. It doesn't have long lists of synonyms, though.

You may be able to get your hands on a second-hand copy of this book, or find it at your local library.

Cryptic Crossword Dictionary Website

This website (bestforpuzzles.com/cryptic-crossword-dictionary/) has a full list of cryptic indicators, listed by cryptic device, as well as lengthy lists of abbreviations, arranged alphabetically by the words you might find in a clue. They also have a nice cryptic crossword tutorial and free puzzles to solve every day (including easy cryptics), which can either be printed out or solved online.

OneLook and Word Navigator Websites

These two websites (www.onelook.com and wordnavigator.com) have many similar functions, so I'm lumping them in together here. On these sites, you can find word definitions and perform a wide variety of powerful wildcard searches. Both sites are valuable tools for solving crosswords of any variety.

On the *OneLook* site, you can limit your results to a particular theme or subject, which can be very helpful. The *WordNavigator* site can identify synonyms and anagrams of words, and lists of words that have similar features to the word you typed in (for example, other words formed from the letters of the word, words starting with the same letter, new words formed from the word by changing one letter and a host of other parameters).

Lovatts You Play Website

This Australian website (www.youplay.com) has a vast variety and number of puzzles, which you can solve for free online. The Lovatts cryptic crossword is a good one for beginners, with an easy rating, and more anagrams and easy clue devices than you find in a newspaper cryptic. The online interface is pleasant to use, and you can get a 'Word Hint' (which reveals the answer to the selected clue) if you're stuck.

The Guardian Website

The website for *The Guardian* newspaper (www.guardian.co.uk/crosswords) has a huge collection of the paper's cryptic crosswords, which you can print out or solve online. Be warned, though, these are full-on British cryptic crosswords, and they do tend to have more Libertarian clues. The Quiptic crossword is designed for beginners but is still rather challenging, so don't feel badly if you can't make sense of it right away!

The Guardian online interface is nice and clear, and has an Anagram function built in. You can use the Cheat function if needs be, to help you get a start on the grid, and check your work as you go.

Although the puzzles on this website are hard, in general, they're definitely puzzles to work towards. You can always work backwards from the answer, nutting out how the clue works, so don't let the difficulty level put you off. I recommend focusing on just one setter or series for starters. Crosswords by Rufus are at the easier end of things.

Sutherland Studios Website

My website (www.sutherland-studios.com.au) has a range of helpful lists of cryptic indicators and abbreviations, handy apps, and free cryptic crosswords to download or solve online. I do my best to add new content regularly.

Chambers Dictionary and Thesaurus Apps

These two apps (available through www.chambers.co.uk) are a bit more expensive than most 'run of the mill' apps, but I've found them to be worth every cent. I use them all the time, for help with both solving and writing cryptic clues. Chambers have a proven track record as the best reference books for crosswords (both quick and cryptic), and their apps live up to this reputation.

The search function is excellent; you can do wildcard searches and even specify vowel/consonant patterns, and then sort your search results by word type (such as nouns, verbs and adjectives). An anagram solver is also included.

Dictionary results not only have full dictionary entries (with pronunciation guides, definitions and word etymologies), but also point out any homophones. The thesaurus entries are extensive.

The dictionary cross-references to the thesaurus or online resources, and vice versa. All English varieties are covered (British, American, Australian and International). No internet connection is required to run the apps, once you've downloaded them.

WordWeb Dictionary App

This is a cut down version of the Chambers dictionary and thesaurus app (refer to the preceding section), with fewer keywords and briefer definitions, but it's completely free. Homophones are identified, as with the Chambers apps, and it has the same excellent search functions. However, it doesn't have the anagram function. But, for the price, it's certainly worth downloading!

WordMaster: Crossword and Anagram Solver App

No free version is available for this app (available at www. trancreative.com), but it's inexpensive. I like this app because it combines the two features that you generally need to solve cryptic clues — a wildcard search and an anagram solver. It also gives letter point scores for the results, so you can use it when playing other word games like Scrabble or Words With Friends.

This app doesn't provide lists of synonyms or definitions for words within the app. Clicking on a word takes you to an online search, which provides a definition for that word, but you need an internet connection for this feature.

CrypticGuide App

This is my own app that provides a searchable cryptic dictionary, as well as a wildcard solver, anagram solver, and hidden word feature. Search for 'CrypticGuide', or my name, on the Apple App Store. It works offline, so is perfect for help cracking cryptics when you're on the go.

Appendix

Word Lists

This Appendix has a great bunch of reference lists that I've put together for you, which can help you on your cryptic journeys. Abbreviations are one of the absolute basic elements of cryptics clues — every crossword uses them — and this list introduces some of the more common ones. I've also included some handy lists of foreign words sometimes used in cryptic clues — French, German, Italian and Spanish are the languages most often used. There is also a list of some anagram indicators.

Appreciating Abbreviations

In the following sections I introduce you to the vast realm of cryptic abbreviations. Many of these are quite common abbreviations that you will be familiar with, but there are just as many that are, shall we say, rather *odd* (and that's me being nice!).

Covering common abbreviations

Any dictionary lists standard abbreviations, like Latin terms, Roman numerals, Greek letters, country licence plate codes and chemical symbols, so I have only included a few examples from these categories in Table A-1. Look up the single letter entries in a dictionary to get a good list of standard abbreviations for that letter. There are also several websites devoted to abbreviations, just search online. Refer to Chapter 18 for resources you can use for longer lists of common abbreviations.

TABLE A-1 **Common Abbreviations by Category**

Chemical symbols	Country codes	Cricketing terms	Greek letters	Latin terms	Roman numerals
calcium = CA	Australia = AUS, AU or OZ	batting = IN	CHI	and so on = ETC	1 = I
gold = AU	Belgium = BEL or BE	bowled = B	ETA	around, about, approx. = C, CA	5 = V
helium = HE	Egypt = ET	caught = C	IOTA	for example, say = EG	6 = VI
hydrogen = H	Greece = GRC, GR or GRE	duck = O (no runs)	MU	in this matter, concerning, about = RE	10 = X
lead = PB	India = IND or IN	innings = I	NU	morning = AM	50 = L
nitrogen = N	Japan = J	maiden = M	PHI	note well = NB	51 = LI
potassium = K	New Zealand = NZL or NZ	no ball = NB	PI	per annum = AP	100 = C
silver = AG	Switzerland = CHE, CH, SUI or SWI	not out = NO	PSI	present day = AD	150 = CL
tellurium = TE	United Kingdom = GBR or UK	over = O	RHO	see = CF	500 = D
uranium = U	United States = USA or US	run = R	TAU	that is = IE	501 = DI
vanadium = V	Yugoslavia = YU	wicket = W	XI	thus = SIC	1,000 = M

Working out weird and wonderful abbreviations

Here I provide a *short* list of just some of the thousands of abbreviations used in cryptic crosswords. Abbreviations are generally used to indicate one or two letters, but occasionally more. Crossword dictionaries and websites devoted to cryptic crosswords have more complete lists (refer to Chapter 18 for my resource recommendations).

a follower = B (alphabet!)

about = C, CE, RE

academic = BA, MA, MB

account = AC

ace = AI (as in A1, but numeral 1 is read as letter I)

against = V, VS (versus)

alien = ET (for extraterrestrial)

alpha = A (phonetic alphabet)

alto = A (singing voice)

American soldier = GI

ancient city = UR

ancient times = BC, BCE

Anglo Saxon = AS

answer = A

Arabic = AR

article = A, AN, THE

artists = RA (for Royal Academy)

Asian = E (Eastern)

at home = IN

bachelor = BA or B

bass = B (singing voice)

beginner = L (for L-plate on a car)

bend = S or U (for S-bend, U-bend)

big = OS (outsized)

bill = IOU

bishop = B (chess)

blood group = A, B, AB, O

bob = S (for shilling)

Bond's boss = M

books = OT, NT (for Old Testament, New Testament)

bravo = B (phonetic alphabet)

bridge player = N, S, E, W (seating)

British = B

Capone = AL

carbon copy = CC

care of = CO

castle = R (see *rook*)

Catholic = C

century = C

chapter = C, CH

Charlie = C (phonetic alphabet)

Christ = X

church = CH, CE (Church of England)

circle, circuit = O

civil engineer = CE

clef = C, F (music)

club/s = C (cards)

Common Era = CE

conservative = C

credit = CR

cross = X

current = AC, DC

Cyprus = CY

daughter = D

day = D or V (Victory Day)

degree = BA (Bachelor of Arts), MA (Master of Arts), D, C or F (for temperature degrees)

delta = D (phonetic alphabet)

diamond/s = D (cards)

direction = N, S, E, W (compass directions)

disc = O (it looks like a circle or disc!), LP, CD

doctor = DR, MD, MB (Bachelor of Medicine), MO (medical officer), GP (general practitioner), DOC

dollar = S (looks like the $ sign)

east/ern = E

echo = E (phonetic alphabet)

egg = O (similar shape)

Elizabeth = ER (from Elizabetha Regina)

energy = E

engineer = CE (civil engineer), RE (Royal Engineers)

English = E

era = AD, BC

excellent = AI (see *ace*)

exercise = PE (physical education), PT (physical therapy)

exist = BE

fine = F (pencil), OK

firm = CO (company)

first class = A or AI (see ace)

first = IST (looks like 1st)

first character = A

first woman = EVE

fish = LING, EEL, COD, GAR, RAY etc.

following = F

footnote = PS

force = F

former = EX

forte = F (music)

foxtrot = F (phonetic alphabet)

French = F

Friday = F, FRI

gas = CO (carbon monoxide), HE (helium) etc

George = G

Georgia = GA (state) or GE (country)

German = G

gold = AU, OR (heraldry)

golf = G (phonetic alphabet)

good = G, A (as in A Grade)

good man = ST (saint)

graduate = BA, MA, MB

grand = G, K (thousand)

Guevara = CHE

hand = AB (see sailor), L (left hand), R (right hand)

hard = H (pencil lead)

heart/s = H (cards)

Her Majesty = HM

hesitation = ER, UM

high class = AI (see *ace*)

high class = U (from upper class)

honour = OBE

hotel = H (phonetic alphabet)

hour = H, HR

hug = O (looks like a hug!)

husband = H

I am = IM (I'm)

in charge = IC

India = I (phonetic alphabet)

island = I or IS

journalist = ED (editor)

judge = J

Juliet = J (phonetic alphabet)

key = A, B, C, D, E, F, G (as in musical keys)

kilo = K (phonetic alphabet)

king = ER (*Edwardus Rex*), R (*Rex*), K (chess)

kiss = X

knight = N (chess)

last character = Z

liberal = L

Lima = L (phonetic alphabet)

line = L (lower case L looks like a line)

loud = F (forte, or loud in music)

love = O (tennis score of zero)

male = M

master = M

measure = EN, EM

midday = N (noon)

Mike = M (phonetic alphabet)

minute = M

model = T (for Model T Ford)

moment = MO

monarch = ER (see *queen*)

Monday = M, MON

monsieur = M

months = MOS

new = N

nil = O

no good = NG

north/ern = N

not applicable = NA

note = A, B, C, D, E, F, G (as in musical notes), DO, RE, MI, FA, SO, LA, TI, DOH, SOH, LAH, or reference to money

nothing = O

November = N (phonetic alphabet), NOV

novice = L (learner)

number = N, NO, PIN (as you'd use at an ATM), or any Roman numeral

number one = ADAM, I (1)

ocean = O

old = O

old boy = OB

old city = UR

Old English = OE

one = I, A, AN, I (1)

operation = OP

oriental = E (from the East)

Oscar = O (phonetic alphabet)

outsize, large, huge = OS (outsized)

page = P

pages = PP

pair = PR

papa = P (phonetic alphabet)

pawn = P (chess)

penny = P

physical education = PE

physical training = PT

playing, performing = ON

point = N, S, E, W

pole = N (north), S (south)

policeman = PC

post office = PO

power = P

present day = AD

princess = DI

printer's measure = EN, EM

private = GI (soldier)

quarter = N, S, E, W

Quebec = Q (phonetic alphabet)

queen = ER (*Elizabetha Regina*), R (*Regina*), Q (chess)

question = Q, QU

quiet = P, PP (from music), SH (sssh!), MUM

railway = RY, BR (British Rail)

ring = O (looks like a ring)

river = R

road = RD

Romeo = R (phonetic alphabet)

rook = R (chess)

roughly = C, CA (circa)

round = O

Royal Navy = RN

sailor = TAR, AB (for able-bodied seaman), OS (ordinary seaman)

sailors = ABS, RN (Royal Navy)

saint = ST

salt = AB (see sailor)

Saturday = S, SAT

scholar = BA

second = S

second class = B

ship = SS

short time = T (the word time shortened)

Sierra = S (phonetic alphabet)

silence = SH, MUM

six-footer = ANT, BEE, etc (an insect has six legs)

society = S

soft = P (piano, which is quiet or soft in music), B (pencil lead)

soldier = GI, RM (Royal Marines)

son = S

soprano = S (singing voice)

south/ern = S

spade/s = S (cards)

square = S

state = any USA state abbreviation

street = ST, AVE, RD, WAY

strings = E, A, D, (violin strings)

student = L (learner)

Sunday = S, SUN

support = BRA

tango = T (phonetic alphabet)

tar = AB (see sailor)

teas = TT (with a 'sounds like' indicator)

teetotal/ler = TT

temperature = T

ten = IO (looks like 10)

tenor = T (singing voice)

text = MS (for manuscript)

thanks = TA

the thing = IT

Thursday = TH, THURS

times = X (multiplication sign)

top class = AI (A1)

translator = TR

Tuesday = T, TU, TUES

Turkey = TR

turn = U (U-turn)

two = DUO, II

uniform = U (phonetic alphabet)

university = U, OU (Open University)

unknown = X (unknown in equations)

upper class = U (rather dated!)

variable = X

versus = V, VS

very = V

very black = BB (pencil)

very loud = FF (fortissimo, very loud in music)

very soft = PP (pianissimo, very soft in music)

victor = V (phonetic alphabet)

vitamin = A, B, C, D, E, BI (B1), etc.

volt = V

volume = V

vote = X

Wednesday = W, WED

week = W

west = W

whiskey = W (phonetic alphabet)

wide/width = W

wife = W

without = WO

woman's supporter = BRA

worker = ANT, BEE

x-ray = X (phonetic alphabet)

Yankee = Y (phonetic alphabet)

year = Y, YR

you (archaic/old) = YE

yours truly = I

Zulu = Z (phonetic alphabet)

Fossicking for Foreign Words

Some foreign words are commonly seen in cryptic crossword clues. In general, the answers are words you may already know, and they tend to be very short words. French, in particular, is used a fair bit.

Very occasionally, a hard cryptic clue may require that you translate a less common word, such as a colour, food or season; in this case, you may need to use a translating dictionary or (easiest of all) use an online translator or vocabulary list for that language.

TIP

If you type 'Translate *x* into *y*' into your search engine of choice (where *x* is the word to be translated and *y* is the language to be changed into), the search results give you an immediate answer (without you having to go to another website).

French

Here's a list of the French words commonly used in cryptic crosswords.

a, the, articles	UN, UNE, LA, LE or LES	king	ROI
and	ET	man, men	M (Monsieur), MM (Messieurs)
art	ES (from I am, thou **art** – Je suis, tu **es**!)	me	MOI
		no	NON
at, in, to	AU	not	PAS
dance	BAL	of	DE, DES, DU
dry	SEC	on	SUR
from, of	DE, DU, DES	one	UN, UNE
girl, Miss	MLLE (Mademoiselle)	said, say	DIT
gold	OR	sea	MER
		she	ELLE
good	BON	street	RUE
he	IL	that	CA, CELA
I	JE	this	CE
in	EN	very	TRES
is	EST	water	EAU
we	NOUS	woman	MME (Madame)
what	QUE	word	MOT
where	OU	yes	OUI
wine	VIN	you	TU, VOUS

German

German words seen in cryptics include the following.

a, an	EIN, EINE, EINER	she	SIE
and	UND	the, this, that	DER, DIE,DAS
gent	HERR	they	SIE
he	ER	we	WIR
I	ICH	where	WO
it	ES	with	MIT
no	NEIN	yes	JA
one	EIN	you	DU, SIE

Italian

Cryptic crosswords may use Italian words, including some of the common ones listed here.

a, an	UN, UNO, UNA	I was	ERO
articles	IL	not	NON
but	MA	of the	DEL
east	EST	one	UNA, UNO
hi	CIAO	six	SEI
I	IO	some	DEI, DELLE
if	SE	south	SUD
the	IL	who	CHI
three	TRE	yes	SI
two	DUE	you	TU

Spanish

Spanish words commonly used in cryptic crosswords include the following.

a, an	UN, UNA	my	MI
articles	EL, LA, LAS, LOS	nobleman	DON
exclamation	OLE	one	UNO
gentleman	DON	that	ESE, ESA
good	BIEN	thousand	MIL
goodbye	ADIOS	three	TRES
hero	CID (El Cid)	two	DOS
I	YO	what	QUE
I am	SOY	yes	SI
man	HOMBRE	you, your	TU

Analysing Anagram Indicators

Anagram indicators are words and short phrases that indicate that some of the other words in a clue (the fodder) have to be jumbled up to make another word (the answer).

Any words that give a sense of words or letters being jumbled, broken, rearranged, disordered, stressed, active, drunk, mixed, constructed, sick, cooked, wrong and so on can be used as anagram indicators — so the full list of all possibilities is immensely long (and possibly infinite)!

This list includes all the anagram indicators used in the clues in this book. Other forms of these words can also be used (that is, present and past tense verbs, nouns, adjectives, adverbs, gerunds and so on).

abnormal	accidentally	adjusted
absurdly	acrobatic	agile
abused	active	agitated

all at sea	broken	dashing
almost	broth	deformed
animated	burst	deliriously
around	busily	demolished
arrange	by mistake	deranged
askew	carelessly	designed
at random	cavorting	destroy
awkward	change	deviant
awry	chaotic	devilish
bad/ly	chopped	disarrayed
baffled	cocktail	disjointed
bananas	confused	disorderly
battered	construction	disorganised
batty	contorted	distraught
beat up	converted	distressed
beaten	cooked	disturbed
bend/t	corrupt	dizzily
bent out of shape	cracked	dodgy
	craftily	drunk
berserk	crazed	dubious
bizarre	crazily	eccentric
blend	crazy	edited
blown up	crooked	elaborate
boiled	crushed	elastic
breaks	damaged	engineer/ed

entangle	harassed	knead
errant	harmed	knocked out
erring	haywire	laboured
erroneous	hectic	lax
erupt	high	liberally
evolved	horribly	lively
excite	horrific	loony
exploded	idiotic	loose
extravagant	imperfect	lunatic
fabricated	improper	mad
fake	in pieces	made up
false	inaccurate	make up
fancy	incorrect	malformed
feign	inebriated	maltreated
fermented	inept	mangled
fishy	injure	manic
flexibly	insanely	mar
fluid	invalid	mash
foolish	irregular	massaged
frantic	irritated	maul
garbled	jazzy	maybe
giddily	jittery	meandering
go off	jostle	meddle
ground	jumble	medley
haphazard	kind of	mélange

melted

messy

mince

misprint

mistakenly

mischievous

mix

mixture

mix-up

mobile

modelled

move

mushy

mutant

nasty

naughty

neatened

new

novel

oddball

oddly

off

organised

ornate

otherwise

out

out of hand

out of place

outrageous

panic

pastiche

peculiar

performing

perhaps

perturb

perverse

pickled

pie

plastered

plastic

playing

poorly

possibly

potty

prancing

prepared

problem

processed

produce

pulverize

puzzling

questionable

quirky

quivering

ragged

rampage

randomly

ravaged

raving

reaction

rearrange

rebuilt

reconfigured

recycled

refined

reformed

remade

remarkable

reorder

repair

resort

restless

rioting	smashed	translated
rocky	somehow	treated
rogue	sort of	trouble
rotten	special	turns
roughly	spoil	twisted
rubbish	spread	ugly
rudely	spurious	uncontrolled
ruin	stew	unexpectedly
rum	stewed	unfamiliar
run wild	stirred	untidy
sadly	stormy	unusual
salad	strangely	upset
scattered	struggling	vaguely
scraggy	surprising	variant
screwed up	swirled	version
sculpture	synthetic	violently
set out	tailor	weird
shaking	tainted	went to pieces
shivering	tangle	whipped
shot	terrible	wild
shuffled	tip over	wobbly
sick	tipsy	wrecked
silly	torn	wriggle
sketchy	torture	zany

About the Author

Denise Sutherland is an Australian author and puzzle writer. She has studied science, graphic design and book indexing. She is a member of the Institute of Professional Editors and ACT Writers Centre.

Denise has been fascinated with puzzles and mysteries of all kinds since she was a child — not surprisingly, murder mysteries are her favourite novels. She has focused on writing puzzles professionally since 2001, and has self-published six puzzle books for children, including the popular *Canberra Puzzle Book*.

This book is Denise's third title in the For Dummies series; her previous books are *Word Searches For Dummies* and *Cracking Codes and Cryptograms For Dummies* (written with Mark Koltko-Rivera). She also enjoys writing non-fiction, especially in the scientific and medical fields. She is the author of *The Patient's Guide to Neurosarcoidosis*, and *A Guide for Adults with Hip Dysplasia*, with Dr Sophie West. Denise blogs at her website, sutherland-studios.com.au, and can be found on Facebook: facebook.com/aussienisi.

Denise lives in Canberra with her astrophysicist husband, two grown-up kids and two mad chihuahuas. She loves knitting, gourmet cooking and solving cryptic crosswords.

Author's Acknowledgements

Firstly, my thanks to my dear family, Ralph, Rodger and Jenny, for their support and help, and for putting up with my ridiculous working hours and addled brain while writing this book.

My gratitude to Alec Robins (sadly no longer with us), for his excellent 1975 book *Teach Yourself Crosswords*, which started me writing cryptic crosswords back in 1992, and is still my favourite reference book. Thanks also to Deborah Green for her help behind the scenes, Ross Beresford, aka Crossword Man, for his excellent *Wordplay Wizard* software, and Greg Parker for his moral support and advice.

Lastly, thanks to Trent Reznor, whose music kept me going!

Publisher's Acknowledgements

We're proud of this book; please send us your comments through our online registration form located at www.dummies.com/register.

Some of the people who helped bring this book to market include the following:

Acquisitions, Editorial and Media Development

Project Editor: Charlotte Duff

Acquisitions Editors: Rebecca Crisp, Clare Weber

Technical Editor: David Stickley

Editorial Manager: Danielle Karvess

Production

Proofreader: Pamela Dunne